SANDHURST

ALAN SHEPPERD

SANDHURST

The Royal Military Academy Sandhurst
and its Predecessors

COUNTRY LIFE BOOKS

Published by Country Life Books
and distributed for them by
The Hamlyn Publishing Group Limited
London · New York · Sydney · Toronto
Astronaut House, Feltham, Middlesex, England

First published 1980
ISBN 0 600 38251 6

Set in 12 on 13·5pt Monophoto Ehrhardt by
Tradespools Limited, Frome

Printed and bound in England by
Hazell, Watson & Viney Limited, Aylesbury

CONTENTS

ACKNOWLEDGEMENTS

This history of Sandhurst and its predecessors inevitably owes much to the work of authors who have trodden the same path in earlier times. In particular I wish to acknowledge my gratitude to Brigadier Sir John Smyth, VC, whose excellent *Sandhurst*, published eighteen years ago, has been a constant companion, source of reference and inspiration.

In my turn I owe a considerable debt to very many people: brother officers; former colleagues at the RMA Sandhurst; ex-cadets, representative of many generations going back to well before the First World War; and all those who have written of their experiences, sent photographs, or allowed themselves to be interviewed, and in so many other ways given me encouragement and support.

Of all those who have helped me in the preparation of this book I am particularly indebted to: Major General Sir Philip Ward, who has given me every encouragement over the last three years; and the following members of his staff: Colonel R.W.H. Crawford, Major N. Gulliver, the Adjutant Major W.H.M. Ross and Academy Sergeant Major R.P. Huggins, together with Lieutenant Colonel M.H. Broadway, Lieutenant Colonel J.R. Roberts and the Academic Registrar Mr B.T. Jones; and also to Mr J.C. Andrews, Chief Librarian, Ministry of Defence Library Services; Mr J.W. Hunt, Librarian, Central Library, the RMA Sandhurst; Mr K.M. White, Librarian, the Staff College, Camberley; Brigadier R.J. Lewendon, the Royal Artillery Institution Library; the Secretary, the Civil Service Commission; and their respective staffs.

Of those who have generously supplied valuable background material and personal accounts I am particularly indebted to: Colonel B.J. Amies; Major General R.E. Aserappa; Lieutenant Colonel M.S. Close; Colonel H.N. Clowes; Lieutenant Colonel P.A.C. Don; Major R.F. Eyles; Lieutenant Colonel K.W. Ferrier; Flight Lieutenant Kip Gilpin; Lieutenant Colonel H.M. Harvey-Jamieson; Mrs Ruth Hicks; the late Brigadier O.F.G. Hogg; Brigadier W.J. Jervois; Major General R.C.M. King; the late Major John Lynch; Major General R.B. Pargiter; Lieutenant Colonel M.A. Philp; Colonel R.A. Rushbridge; Major C. Salmon; Major H. Skillen; Brigadier W.H.D. Wakely; Major General M.C. Wheatley; and Lieutenant Colonel J.K. Windeatt.

I would especially like to thank Dr T.A. Heathcote, the Curator of the RMA Sandhurst Collection, for his invaluable assistance over the illustrations; Mr P.A. Warner for much helpful advice; Mrs P.G. Brooking and Mrs D.L. Gair, who have given much time and attention to typing the manuscript; Mr M.G.H. Wright, the Deputy Librarian at Sandhurst, for his most valued assistance with the index; and finally my wife Lesley, but for whose patience and support these words would not have been written.

Preface

This is the story of Sandhurst, of its antecedents, and of its evolution over a period of some two hundred and fifty years to become our sole officer-cadet training establishment for the British Army. Here we see the emergence of the Royal Military Academy Sandhurst into modern times and trace its origins, traditions and progress, while briefly glimpsing the work and life of successive generations of cadets and those who have taught them. This account, however, neither pretends nor claims to be an official history. Much of the framework must be predetermined, but the avenues of research and the choice of material have been largely dictated by personal choice.

This has been a voyage of discovery, navigated through waters that in the past were often poorly charted, that were sometimes calm and peaceful, but more often were darkened by gathering clouds and swept by the driving urgency of war. Here we retrace a passage, a progress from the earliest days, that in recent times has become increasingly subject to external pressures, to the ebb and flow of changing and sometimes vacillating policies and the shifting sands that bedevil the contemporary economic scene. Thus the underlying theme may be seen as a study of the pattern of change, which in turn may point to some of those stabilising influences that may support the Sandhurst of the future in its vital tasks.

Camberley   Alan Shepperd
1979

CHAPTER 1

A Fledgling Academy

'SERVE TO LEAD'

The badge worn by the officer cadets of the Royal Military Academy Sandhurst bears the motto 'Serve to Lead', an exhortation that is equally a profession of faith and dedication for all aspirants to the Queen's Commission as members of the officer corps of the British Army. Implicit is the concept of the family, of the ties that bind men of single purpose, joined together by those close and intangible links that unite members of the unit, the regiment, the corps, the Army itself. Retrospectively, as in any family, heredity, custom, tradition and the ties of marriage become salient factors in an evolutionary process, giving roots, strength and a sense of unity to succeeding generations.

The story of modern RMA Sandhurst properly has a beginning and a middle, but the third and present element, inevitably caught up in the ebb and flow of a continually developing process, can only be held in momentary focus. So to bring the present into a wider perspective we must not only take a backward glance at the first hesitant steps in the setting up of the Royal Military Academy at Woolwich and later the Royal Military College at Sandhurst, looking at the early evolution of these two great military institutions, we must also trace the succeeding stages of their development up to modern times and their eventual amalgamation. Only then will the contemporary scene of a single college, the RMA Sandhurst, be set against its proper historical background.

TOWER PLACE AND THE ROYAL ACADEMY

The early history of the Royal Academy, as the RMA Woolwich was initially called, is closely associated with the Warren, which from 1671 formed the nucleus of the Royal Arsenal. This Thames-side estate of some thirty-one acres (12.5 ha) was in that year made the subject of an order in council and acquired by the Board of Ordnance. The estate included 'the great mansion or Manor House called the Tower Place' and a number of warehouses and workshops, and was described as 'a convenient place for

9

building a storehouse for powder and other stores of war, and for room for the proof of guns'. Tower Place, a substantial Tudor mansion on three floors, built over a hundred years previously, was soon converted to provide accommodation for the Master Gunner of England and the Storekeeper for the Arsenal. Later, between 1718 and 1720, it was virtually rebuilt by Sir John Vanbrugh. Behind a new façade two large rooms were constructed on either side of the main entrance. The Great Room was for the use of the Board of Ordnance and opposite was an equally large room to provide for an academy. In addition there was to be a house for a 'mathematical' master.

The decision to construct the second large room was made while the rebuilding was actually in progress and is linked with the formation of the Royal Regiment of Artillery four years previously and the need 'for educating youth and improving the officers of the artillery and engineers in their respective duties'. The close links between the Academy and the adjacent workshops mentioned above is generally considered to be the reason why the RMA Woolwich became known as 'the Shop'.

The number of young students at the start was small, but the place they held in the newly established regiment was obviously of some importance. In the four years of its existence the Regiment's strength had nearly doubled to a little under four hundred all ranks, the majority of whom were under training at Woolwich. Moreover, the establishment included twenty young men enlisted as cadet gunners and cadet matrosses, or gunners' mates.

The master appointed to teach mathematics to the cadets, 'on such days and at such times as did not interfere with other service duties', was a Mr Burnett Godfrey. Godfrey's rank at the time was that of fireworker, i.e. a specialist in the manufacture of explosives and military types of fireworks. Now he found himself commissioned, and later given the rank of second lieutenant in one of the marching (or training) companies, with the unenviable task of teaching the wild and unruly batch of cadets, who very likely took exception to being 'stopped £4 a year towards gratifying the said Mr Godfrey or such other officers who shall instruct them in gunnery and fortification'.

How long this experimental regimental school lasted we do not know, only that Godfrey's name does not appear in the regimental records after 1731. Nor was a successor appointed. For the reason we have not far to look, as only a few years later the commanding officer at Woolwich noted in the muster roll that of the sixteen cadets only two were in the station. Four were on detachment and against the remaining names was the remark 'I know not where they are!' But the long years of peace that had lasted since the days of Marlborough were over. Following the quarrel with Spain in 1739 and the outbreak of the War of the Austrian Succession, a shortage of officers persuaded the Board of Ordnance to reopen the Academy.

The Master General at this time was John, Duke of Montagu, a general in the Army, privy councillor and a cousin of George II. His 'representation . . . that it would conduce to the good of Our Service if an academy or school was instituted, endowed and supported for instructing the raw and inexperienced people belonging to the Military Branch of this Office [of Ordnance], in the several parts of mathematicks necessary to qualify them for the service of the Artillery, and the business of Engineers', received the royal approval on 30 April 1741. The Academy was to be established in the 'convenient room' in Tower Place, and the annual budget, which was to include the salaries of 'an able and skilful master and assistants', was fixed at £500. The appointment of two masters followed in July and that of a secretary in September. After a pause of some weeks, the 'Rules and Orders for the Royal Academy at Woolwich', together with a detailed syllabus, were issued. As the salaries of the three civilian staff now took up all but a hundred pounds of the money voted, everyone concerned must have been greatly relieved that the Master General had meanwhile succeeded in doubling the annual grant.

THE COURSE IN 1741

Once again the intention was that the Academy should serve as the regimental school. Over and above the cadets (the number in 1742 was about thirty), all commissioned and non-commissioned officers not required for duty, together with such bombardiers, miners, pontoonmen, matrosses and others as were capable of absorbing the instruction, were required to attend the lectures on 'theory'. Three days in each week were thus occupied, with the chief master lecturing in the morning from 8 to 11 a.m. (winter times were an hour later) and the second master from 3 to 6 p.m. The syllabus was based on the study of mathematics, to include trigonometry and conic sections, and such aspects of mechanics, physics and chemistry as were required by eighteenth-century artillery and engineering techniques. Since there were no textbooks, notes had to be taken down in writing as dictated, and a duty officer, not below the rank of lieutenant, had to be present to keep order.

The 'practice' was taught on the remaining three days of the week. This part of the syllabus covered the whole spectrum of training in gunnery, fortification, bridge-building, mining and magazine techniques, together with instruction on the detailing, setting-up and supply of a train of artillery. This work was directed by the Commanding Officer of Artillery at Woolwich, who detailed suitable instructors, while the two masters lectured on the principles involved. In wet weather the time was to be devoted to instruction in the making of gunpowder and precautions in its use, together with fireworks, 'whether for the annoyance of the enemy or for public rejoicings'. Part of each summer was to be given over either to building fortifications or, in the words of the syllabus, setting up an attack 'with all the form and regularity that is used in a real siege'. Finally, it was laid down that each year there would be a 'general examination as well as a great and solemn exercise of Artillery', attended by the Master General and the whole Board of Ordnance, and that at the latter exercise a 'prize of honour' would be presented to the best in each of the three classes of 'learners', divided in modern terms into the good, average and indifferent.

THE MASTERS

The chief master was Martin Folkes, the recently appointed President of the Royal Society, with which august body the Academy later became closely associated. Folkes was also a close friend of the Duke of Montagu and it seems that his post was held as a sinecure. Pocketing the salary of £200 per annum, he never occupied the official residence at Tower Place and rarely, if ever, visited Woolwich. Instead he employed Mr John Muller, a lowly paid mathematical instructor in the drawing office of the Tower, to deliver his lectures.

In fact the fledgling Academy was struggling to survive the first few years of its reincarnation, and this in spite of its grandiose title, comprehensive syllabus and professional staff. In the flurry and bustle of the Regiment's expansion the problems of the two masters had hardly been considered and they faced an almost impossible task. The disparity in rank, age and education of the 'learners' produced confusion enough, but the essential element, that of discipline, was almost totally lacking. Those affected most were of course the young and immature cadets. These youthful aspirants to a commission, whose average age was between twelve and fourteen, were only too willing to ape the wild and intemperate habits of the young officers of the garrison. Required to find their own lodgings in the town, the cadets found themselves freed of any kind of supervision out of working hours, while during classes there was such a state of fracas that the presence of the orderly officer was constantly in demand to quell the noise and brawling and stop the pelting of the hard-pressed masters.

The Company of Gentlemen Cadets

During the summer of 1744 HRH The Duke of Cumberland went down to Woolwich to attend some experiments and a proof, and could hardly have failed to take note of the twenty or so cadets who were paraded separately without uniforms or arms. Perhaps their unmilitary appearance on such a formal occasion met with royal displeasure, or the commanding officer may have had a tactful word with the Master General. Whatever the case, action quickly followed. Within a matter of weeks a royal warrant was issued setting up a separate Company of Gentlemen Cadets (as they were now to be called) under a captain, three other officers and a drum major. The establishment of gentlemen cadets was fixed at forty by taking five from each of the Regiment's marching companies. All were to be paid 1s. 4d. a day, which was a rise of 4d. for the cadet matrosses. The annual cost to public funds was now £1,645. 10s. 10d. for the service pay of the

Tower Place, the first home of the Royal Military Academy. To the left is Prince Rupert's Tower. From a painting by Paul Sandby, appointed Drawing Master in 1768. Royal Library, Windsor Castle.

Cadet Company, plus the £1,000 voted for the running of the Academy itself.

The central problem, however, remained unsolved. While the cadets could now be paraded under their own officers for practical purposes, an obvious advantage with regard to the military instruction, the Academy itself was still being used as a regimental school. Nor was there any question of Lord Montagu delegating any of his responsibilities for the overall control. On his death in 1749 we find that Sir John Ligonier, the Lieutenant General of Ordnance, became captain of the Company of Gentlemen Cadets. In active command was a regimental officer, a captain who was paid £1. 3s. 6d. a day. This was just about double the combined pay of the three other commissioned officers on the strength of the company. There is no doubt that they all earned every penny. So long as the war in Europe continued and the fighting in India and North America, the pressure on the company officers to bring the more mature and advanced cadets up to the mark in the practical business of gunnery and engineering would have kept them more than fully occupied, leaving the civilian staff of the Academy virtually unsupported to get along with the remainder as best they could.

COLONEL BELFORD TAKES CHARGE

During the Flanders campaign one of the officers who had come to the fore was William Belford, and in 1748, after the Peace of Aix-la-Chapelle, he was back in quarters in the Warren as Lieutenant Colonel of the Regiment. Belford was a man of stature, an enthusiastic gunner with recent experience of command in the field and in particular a considerable reputation as a disciplinarian. The uneasy peace in Europe brought an immediate reduction in the size of the Army, but in 1755 General Braddock's column was destroyed near the banks of the Ohio. Within the decade, with the outbreak of the Seven Years War, twenty new regiments had been raised, together with a Company of Miners – the forerunners of the Corps of Royal Engineers. As for the Royal Artillery, over the same period no less than ten new companies were formed. Meanwhile at Woolwich Colonel Belford had set about injecting a new spirit into the Regiment, and he could hardly have failed to note the need for the work of the Academy to be more closely supervised. In this he was actively supported by Sir John Ligonier, for in 1753 we find that, over and above his other duties, Belford was given the appointment of Assistant and Clerk to the Royal Academy, a post that previously had been held by a civilian. This was the first attempt to place the Academy on a military footing.

14

THE ACADEMY IN THE 1750S

In 1752 the whole company was accommodated in a new barrack block, built on the edge of the regimental parade ground. The establishment of cadets was now forty-eight, including four corporals. With military discipline easier to apply, as Brigadier Hogg writes (in *The Royal Arsenal*), 'the subjection of the cadets had begun'. Nor were the young officers who attended the Academy excluded, as one of Colonel Belford's orders shows:

That no officer lately made, or to be made, go to the Academy unless, it is to study themselves under the instruction of the different masters; and shall any officer, after this order is given, interrupt or otherwise disturb the cadets, in the Academy, the officer who is on duty is to order the person or persons so offending to their rooms, and to report him or them to the commanding officer.

The cadets now paraded and marched to church with the Regiment, and each week one of the three company officers was detailed to 'attend constantly the school hours, to eat in barracks [and] attend at the meals regularly'. He also had to ensure that 'the orderly corporal called the roll at breakfast, dinner, supper and tattoo; after which the barrack door to be locked, viz. at 10 o'clock in summer and 9 in winter; the officer to keep the key till the next morning'. Any cadet who left the Warren or broke out of the barracks after tattoo had been sounded, calling all troops to their quarters, faced dismissal.

The barrack accommodation was built to a minimum standard of comfort and usage, characteristic of an age that expected much of the Army and gave little in return. Up to eight cadets shared a room and over the next twenty years they slept two in a bed. No recreation room was provided and at least one pastime was actively discouraged by Colonel Belford's notable order, issued no doubt for the best of reasons: 'The first cadet swimming in the Thames shall be taken out naked and put in the guard room.' One concession was the appointment of a fencing master, who attended on two days a week and was also required to instruct any officer of the garrison who cared to attend the class.

PATTISON, THE FIRST LIEUTENANT GOVERNOR

In 1764 Lieutenant General the Marquis of Granby, a privy councillor and Colonel of the Horse Guards, was in the first year of his appointment as Master General of the Ordnance. The captain lieutenant of the Cadet Company at this time was Lieutenant Colonel James Pattison, the experienced and highly regarded commanding officer of the 3rd Battalion, who earlier in his career had held the appointment of chief fireworker at

The Cadet Barracks in the Warren, Woolwich Arsenal – showing preparations for the start of the summer vacation. Records of the RMA.

the Woolwich Laboratory. Seeking to 'regulate' the whole function and work of the Academy, Granby created a new appointment, that of Lieutenant Governor, and promoted Pattison into what was virtually an unassailable position of authority to carry out a whole range of reforms.

There was to be a new name – the Royal Military Academy; new rates of pay for the cadets – 2s. 6d. a day; an additional master; a standard weekly timetable with set subjects, covering six hours a day, six days a week; and the Academy was to be entirely reserved for the instruction of the gentlemen cadets. The professors and masters were to reside at Woolwich and were forbidden to take private pupils without the Master General's express permission, and the cadets were to be divided into four classes. The morning and afternoon sessions, each of three hours, were to be taken in turn by the two professors (lecturing on fortification and artillery, and mathematics) and the drawing and French masters.

The newly appointed master for classics, writing and common arithmetic, the Reverend William Green, had the unenviable task of teaching the 'infant' class on three complete days a week, in lieu of their attending the lectures on the art and science of war by the two professors. Where these youthful dullards were taught is not certain, as the Academy was still using the original room in Tower Place, but it was probably in the Board Room across the corridor. The Board Room was already in occasional use for staging amateur dramatics performed by the cadets, and a few years later was fitted up with desks as the Lower School. Incidentally both Mr Green and the French master, who were each paid £40 a year, received less than the two model-makers on the staff and the cadets they taught. Pattison as Lieutenant Governor received £200 a year, as did John Muller, the newly styled 'Professor of Fortifications and Artillery'. Muller had now served twenty-five years at the Academy and must have received some satisfaction from having two of his books, *Elements of Fortification* and *Attack on Fortified Places*, officially nominated as required textbooks.

Without laying down a minimum age for joining, new 'Rules for the Company of Gentlemen Cadets' specified that a 'legal certificate of age' would be required and that on appointment the cadet must 'join the Company, reside at Woolwich and attend the Academy'. It is evident that Pattison, who probably drafted the rules himself, had put his finger on a delicate area of privileged indulgence emanating from the office of the Master General. On his sending out joining orders to seven cadets, who it seems had been given permission to absent themselves until reaching the age of twelve, Pattison discovered that only one would be eligible to join within the following two years and the three youngest would be officially absent for the next six to nine years. The very youngest, Edward Morrison, was in fact three years old!

Domestic affairs also came in for close attention. For some years Pattison had been battling to improve the lot of Mrs Elizabeth James, an officer's widow who acted as housekeeper. Garret windows had been fitted for her apartment in the roof of the cadet barracks, and more recently a much needed pantry and coal-store had been provided. Now she was allocated a monthly budget to be set against a standard diet sheet. Every cadet on the establishment was to contribute 9*d.* a day, and those in residence paid an extra 3*d.* a day for their board. She was also to receive 2*s.* a day towards the expenses of two housemaids and 9*d.* a day for boarding each of the three menservants. The weekly diet to be provided was: breakfast – bread and milk, milk porridge or water-gruel; dinner – beef or mutton and one vegetable served hot, with an apple or fruit pie once a week; supper – bread and cheese on five nights and bread and butter on two nights, or (optimistically!) cold meat left over at dinner. For Sunday dinner there was to be roast veal, and on alternate Saturdays roast pork in season, but followed by roast beef on the Sunday.

Within a few years (by 1772) we find that the deduction from the cadet's pay for boarding had gone up to 1s. a day. The other charges were 6d. a day for clothing; surgeon 8d. and servants 2s., both per month; agency (an administrative surcharge) 3d. in the pound, and for the dancing master 4 guineas a year. This left the cadet with £11. 17s. 6d. out of his annual pay of £45. 12s. 6d.; or just over 7d. a day for what were euphemistically noted as 'necessaries, etc.'

AN INSPECTOR APPOINTED

Altogether Pattison spent eighteen years on the staff of the Academy, the first five in command of the Cadet Company and the remaining years as Lieutenant Governor. Over the whole period he found himself conducting a running battle on two fronts as many of his reforms were equally resisted by both the cadets and professors. Pattison, however, was not a man to shirk responsibility and held to his principles with tenacity, striving at each move to strike at the root of some particular problem.

Fairly soon after his appointment as Lieutenant Governor Pattison felt the need to shield himself from direct personal confrontation with the professors, many of whom resented any form of direction or supervision. The result was the arrival on the staff of Captain George Smith in the new appointment of Inspector, whose duties were constantly to observe and report both on the academic standards and progress of the cadets, as well as on the diligence and teaching practices of the professors and masters. Some of these latter were not only very jealous of retaining their previous freedom to act how they liked, but were only too ready to make the Inspector's task as difficult as possible, and in this they found eager allies in the cadets.

Records of this period give many instances of masters leaving their classes unattended for hours on end, or failing to hand in the monthly progress reports, and sometimes not following the syllabus at all. In the long run, however, the efforts of the Inspector gradually brought improvements which were reflected in the standards achieved in the periodic public examinations. It is significant that the appointment of an Inspector continued for more than a century.

While Captain Smith's presence in and around the Academy curbed some of the more exuberant behaviour of the cadets, there remained a hard core of recalcitrants. Once a cadet had been put under arrest for a particularly serious misdemeanour he was automatically brought before the Lieutenant Governor. In extreme cases Pattison did not hesitate to have the cadet removed by court martial. In one such case referred to the Master General, Pattison describes the two culprits as 'Scabby Sheep . . . capable of corrupting many of their young associates', who had not been

A gentleman cadet of the 2nd (or Lower) Academy in 1783. The blue frockcoat with red facings was worn by that class alone.
Records of the RMA.

brought to heel by 'the punishments we can inflict such as confinement to a dark room, being put on bread and water etc.'

FURTHER REFORMS

In the case of the younger cadets Pattison achieved two important reforms. Firstly, he succeeded in initiating a minimum standard for admission, the requirement being a grounding in the first four rules of arithmetic and a competent knowledge of the 'rule of three' and the elements of Latin grammar. The validity of this request was undoubtedly strengthened by the Master General recently having had to remove a young man who could neither read or write. Secondly, orders were issued that all cadets on joining were to be kept in a subordinate class, i.e. the Lower Academy, until they reached the age of fifteen, or were able to prove, by examination, their ability to enter the Academy proper. They were to be dressed in the simple frockcoat and were not allowed to wear a sword. In their work they were to be confined entirely to academic studies, and on the disciplinary side they were subject to corporal punishment 'without the formality of courts martial'.

Meanwhile the corporals had introduced their own methods of enforcing discipline and matters were brought to a head when the Lieutenant Governor discovered them 'making the gentlemen kneel down on both knees with uplifted hands in the attitude of prayer . . . and other painful and ridiculous postures'. This, he ordered, was to stop immediately, as well as the practice of striking the cadets. Instead the punishments awarded by the corporals were to be restricted to extra guard duty; otherwise misbehaviour was to be reported to the master on duty, who had the option of ordering that the cadet be marched back to barracks and reported in writing to the commanding officer.

Problems in Times of War and Peace

In 1777 Pattison was promoted to Major General and posted to an Army command in America. His successor at the Academy was Colonel Bramham of the Royal Engineers, a corps which for the last sixteen years had been receiving young officers direct from the Academy rather than through the Royal Artillery. Bramham's main concern during these war years was to maintain standards in the face of the constant need for more young officers for the Artillery in particular. Public examinations of the whole Academy were discontinued. Instead batches of selected cadets were examined 'privately' by a board consisting of the Lieutenant Governor, the Inspector and the two senior professors, presided over by a general officer. The appointments following one such board were as follows: of seventeen cadets examined, four received commissions as second lieutenants in the Royal Artillery, five as ensigns in various regiments, and six were sent out to America as volunteers, presumably with the possibility of filling a vacancy in the field.

Over the following twelve months we find fourteen cadets receiving commissions into the Royal Artillery, with three others sent out as volunteers. Two gentlemen attendants and one gentleman of the Tower (a draftsman) were also commissioned. There were, however, ten who failed the examination. Of the gentlemen cadets who became second lieutenants we find that four were aged between fourteen and sixteen. Being judged too young to serve in the Regiment, they were held back to continue their studies for a year or more before joining their companies. At the next examination only half the candidates, all of whom were young, succeeded in passing. Shortly afterwards the Inspector reported that word was going around that the quickest way of getting a commission was to be dismissed from the Academy and obtain one through influence or purchase, as had some former cadets who had been dismissed for 'insufferable crimes'. The result was quite predictable and we find the French master being abused and pelted in class with stones and again attacked on his way home. The suspension of the cadets followed and they were court-martialled. The Master General, however, recommended to His Majesty that they should be reinstated with loss of all seniority and subject to their future good conduct.

At the time of the signing of the Peace of Versailles in 1783 the establishment of the Royal Artillery was 257 officers and 42 companies, totalling 5,337, all ranks. A cutback of 2,000 was immediately ordered, but the Cadet Company, now 60 strong, was left intact. For the next four years, however, no gentlemen cadets were commissioned into the Regiment. Public examinations were now reinstated, but only for cadets 'of very long standing'. The subjects covered were: elements of fortification, attack and defence, construction and tracing of field works, artillery, estimates, surveying and levelling, etc., trigonometry, mensuration, conic sections, hydrostatics, projectiles, mechanics, fluxions and its applications, etc., elements of algebra, quadratic and higher equations, Euclid and chemistry. Military French and drawing, which included 'aerial perspective', were a prerequisite for commissioning.

Major General Pattison was now back in command of the whole of Woolwich, and with little to look forward to but hard study and restrictive regulations, the cadets behaved, if anything, in a worse manner than before. After one particularly 'mutinous' incident, the Duke of Richmond berated the then Lieutenant Governor for not having put the entire Cadet Company under close arrest in the 'common guardroom' for disorderly behaviour.

On a slightly different and individual level, in January 1792 we find 'Mr O., Gentleman Cadet, dismissed for presenting a fowling-piece at a young woman when returning from shooting on Sunday morning, on account of some abusive language she made use of, and after having declared he would shoot her, actually shot, and very much wounded her in the face and breast. Twenty guineas were paid to the father to prevent him sending Mr O. to Maidstone Gaol.' The following year, however, the Master General was concerned more with the 'deficiency so apparent in the studies of the gentlemen cadets' and the resultant difficulty in filling the great number of vacant commissions, for 1793 brought the outbreak of the wars of the French Revolution and the whole of Europe was plunged into violent turmoil.

CHAPTER 2

Le Marchant's Outline

LE MARCHANT

With the outbreak of war against France in 1793 a token British force was hurriedly dispatched under the Duke of York to the Low Countries. One of the cavalry brigades was commanded by General the Hon. William Harcourt, who chose as his brigade major Captain Le Marchant of the 2nd Dragoon Guards. It so happened that each of these three officers was destined to be directly concerned with the establishment of a military school for training officers for the Army, but it was John Gaspard Le Marchant, the youngest and most junior, who formulated the plans and carried them to fruition, thus becoming the founder of the Royal Military College.

Britain, alone amongst the nations drawn into the war, had no military school for her officer corps, no trained staff officers and, except in the case of some Artillery and Engineer officers educated at Woolwich, held firmly to the archaic system of commissioning officers by purchase. This system certainly benefited the Treasury but often produced twelve-year-old ensigns who, if their parents' pockets were deep enough, could become colonels at twenty. Indeed, in the absence of a sizeable private fortune, advancement in the service could well depend on the death of a brother officer, or promotion in the field as a reward for a notable act of gallantry. The other way of advancement was through royal patronage, as all commissions stemmed from the Sovereign.

Le Marchant had few, if any, private means, but with many soldierly qualities (he was a fine horseman and quite exceptional swordsman) and a reputation as an outstanding regimental officer, his talents were soon recognised and he was given a majority in the 16th Light Dragoons. This was on Lord Harcourt's recommendation. Little could he have imagined at that time that Harcourt's patronage would later turn to acrimony and distrust.

On home service in his new regiment, Le Marchant had time to consider lessons he had learned in Flanders. He first of all decided that something must be done to improve the standard of swordsmanship in the cavalry.

Major General Le Marchant. From a drawing by J.D. Harding.

The result was the introduction of an entirely new pattern of sabre to his own design. Officially approved by the Duke of York, now the Commander-in-Chief, this sword was authorised for general issue and remained in service with the light cavalry for the next twenty years. At the same time Le Marchant produced a comprehensive and fully illustrated manual, *Rules and Regulations for the Sword Exercises of the Cavalry*. These 'Exercises' were officially adopted for the training of all cavalry regiments, and the first printing of 1,000 copies sold out in six weeks. Forming a cadre of instructors from his regiment, Le Marchant then embarked on a six months' tour of the country, demonstrating the drills and supervising the setting-up of similar cadres in other regiments.

Somewhat naturally Le Marchant's efforts were favourably noticed at Court as well as at Horse Guards, in the office of the Commander-in-Chief, resulting in his promotion to a lieutenant colonelcy without purchase, and in June 1797, at the age of thirty-one, he joined his new regiment, the 7th Light Dragoons. His days were spent training the regiment, but by rising early and working late he made time in which to produce a *Revision of*

Standing Orders for the Army for the Duke of York, and there followed pamphlets and manuals on every conceivable aspect of cavalry training, as well as schemes for mobilising a Home Guard and organising the Provisional Cavalry against a French invasion. During this period, however, as his son Denis later wrote, his experiences, both in Flanders and on home service, 'all combined to convince him that the real drawback to any essential reform of the Service arose from the officers, and not from the men: so that, until the former were adequately instructed, the character of our armies could never be permanently raised'. The accomplishment of this in the end became Le Marchant's main preoccupation.

PLANS FOR A MILITARY COLLEGE

Fortunately for his country Le Marchant was a man both of vision and with the courage to face up to the existing situation and do something about it. His first thoughts emerged as *A Plan for Establishing Regimental Schools for Officers throughout the Service*, but amongst commanding officers there would be much variance in knowledge and experience, and Le Marchant became convinced that it was only through the setting-up of a single national establishment that his objects could be achieved. But this idea would inevitably arouse public suspicion, as well as the animosity of those officers who might feel that their own positions were under attack. Indeed, when Le Marchant submitted an 'Outline Plan' to the Commander-in-Chief in January 1799, the Duke, while giving his general approval to the scheme, expressed doubts about the possibility of overcoming these prejudices, advising that stronger arguments were needed.

In essence the plan was for a college of three departments. The most junior would be in effect a preparatory school for those aspiring to the King's Commission who had 'finished their classical studies'. The entry age would be between thirteen and fifteen. The second department would carry the instruction forward to the point where, having passed a further two examinations, the cadets would qualify for commissioning. This was a straightforward military course covering both in theory and practice the duties of a subaltern officer, and the syllabus included geometry, trigonometry and military sketching. To provide the framework for the practical side of this instruction there was to be a 'legion', of one cavalry and four infantry companies, recruited from the sons of soldiers. After three years at the college they would return to their regiments, having meanwhile received free education and an excellent grounding in Army discipline and training. The first or most senior department was to be a school where officers of more than four years' service could qualify for staff appointments.

24

In his attempts to persuade influential members of the Government that a military college was urgently needed, Le Marchant had to revise his plans a number of times, particularly with Treasury resistance in mind. From surviving drafts, however, it is clear that he refused to abandon his original ideas for producing better educated officers. These were so novel and regarded in so many quarters as even dangerous that he was forced to advocate, much against his nature, that the project might be carried forward step by step.

It so happened that a French royalist *émigré*, General Jarry, had recently arrived in England. Jarry had an international reputation as an extremely competent staff officer who had served under Frederick the Great and been appointed the first Governor of the Kriegsschule, the military school in Berlin. At the suggestion of the Duke of York he and Le Marchant were brought together. A few months later, in May 1799, a school for training staff officers was set up in temporary accommodation in the Antelope Inn at High Wycombe. Le Marchant was in charge and the ageing General gratefully accepted the subordinate position of Director of Instruction, with an annual salary of £500.

General François Jarry. From a drawing by J.D. Harding.

Le Marchant continued his personal fight for the recognition of what he regarded as the main object of his whole 'Outline', the setting of proper standards of achievement for young officers. These he saw as: a broad education including foreign languages, military training before joining a regiment and qualifying examinations before commissioning.

To enter the Junior Department the candidate would need to be grounded in vulgar fractions, write a good hand and be well acquainted with grammar; and all recommendations should be approved by the Governor of the College. The course should last two or three years and provide a balanced general education with a firm military background. Both French and German would be taught, together with military geography and history (with Persian or Hindustani for the East India Company cadets). The establishment of 200 would be made up of 100 sons of gentlemen, 50 East India Company cadets – all paying 100 guineas a year – and 50 orphans of 'serving officers who had died in His Majesty's Service and in distressed circumstances, or children of officers with large families to maintain on Military Subsistence'. Those in the latter group would enter at the reduced rate of thirty-one guineas a year. Progress throughout the course would be by examination.

Before being accepted into the Second Department of the College the aspiring cadet would first have 'to be approved of by the commanding officer of a regiment, as successor to a vacant commission', and if he wished to enter by purchase, the required sum would have to be lodged with the regimental agent. Candidates for the Cavalry would be required to bring their own chargers and stay six months; those seeking commissions in the Infantry would do a shorter course. All would be required to pay a fee of £36. 12s., to cover the cost of messing and incidental expenses, and the granting of a commission at the end of the course would depend on the cadet passing two examinations.

In his eagerness to gain the co-operation of the Treasury, Le Marchant claimed that, providing the necessary accommodation was provided, the College, with an establishment of 560 (staff and students) in the Junior Department and 355 in the Second Department, would be self-supporting. Indeed, after thirty years the accounts of the Junior Department would show a credit balance of £141,550. 1s. 10½d., while the Second Department should be in credit annually to the tune of £7,921. 0s. 0d. Keeping his proposals for military staff to the minimum, where pay and allowances would have to come from Army funds, Le Marchant estimated that the requirements for civilian staff were as follows: for the 'prep school' twenty-three professors or masters, with a further sixteen for the cadet school. The total number of servants and kitchen staff required would be seventy-nine, and this included clerks. The salaries and wages of all these civilians would be covered by the fees paid by the students, as would all the day-to-day expenses of running the whole College.

THE ROYAL MILITARY COLLEGE ESTABLISHED

Having studied these details, the Duke of York set up a special committee to examine the whole project, which he himself strongly supported, appointing himself its president. In the Committee's report, however, the concept of the legion was turned down 'as being inconsistent with the habits of the country to raise private soldiers to so close an equality with their officers . . . [a] measure which might prove injurious to the Service at large, by leading to frequent promotions from the ranks'. The Committee did go so far as to recommend that a sum of £146,000 should be voted to provide a proper home for the College, which would embrace the staff school already functioning at High Wycombe. This recommendation, optimistically based on Le Marchant's calculations, did not carry any weight with the Treasury, and the only immediate result was an *ex gratia* payment to Le Marchant of £500, accompanied by a complimentary letter from the Secretary of State in recognition of the years of work he had spent on the plans. After months of delay a royal warrant was issued, officially recognising the school at High Wycombe, now to be known as the Royal Military College, and appointing a supreme board for its govern-ance, but with no mention of the other departments.

This half-hearted recognition of all their efforts did little to discourage either the Commander-in-Chief or the architect of the 'Outline', for both were well aware that some 450 acres (182 ha) of land at Sandhurst had already been purchased as a site for the proposed college. Furthermore, a few days before the issue of the royal warrant the Duke of York had on his own initiative opened the Royal Military Asylum in Chelsea for the orphan sons of soldiers. Taking the place of the 'legion', this school later moved to Dover as the now famous Duke of York's Royal Military School.

Encouraged by the interest of the Special Committee, Le Marchant had taken on additional professors at High Wycombe, and when an expedition was mounted to attack the French in Egypt he sent three of the best students to join General Abercromby's staff. The work of these young majors now proved to be a wonderful advertisement for the College and gained wide recognition.

With a change of government since the publication of the Committee's report, and the success of the 'Wycombites', the whole climate of opinion was swinging in favour of Le Marchant's original concept of a national military college. In less than a year a further royal warrant established a Junior Department of the Royal Military College. Rented accommodation was found at Great Marlow, and here the first intake of sixteen gentlemen cadets joined the College on 17 May 1802.

PLANS TO BUILD AT SANDHURST

Meanwhile the recently appointed Supreme Board of the College, under the active presidency of the Commander-in-Chief himself, had not been idle. Plans to house both departments of the College on the Sandhurst estate had already been commissioned from James Wyatt, a well-known architect who was also Surveyor to the Board of Works. The only buildings on the estate were a manor house, with the adjacent farm and mill, that William Pitt had purchased from his niece the Lady Griselda Tekel shortly before the land was acquired by the Government. Wyatt's estimate for the college building was £119,000, with a saving of £14,000 if military labour was used. So it was decided to fit up the manor house as a barrack for an officer and 176 men of the staff corps who would be employed on the construction work.

A Mr Bracebridge was appointed superintendent of the estate, with instructions to plant and lay out the grounds, a task that was completed over the following autumn and winter with considerable imagination and

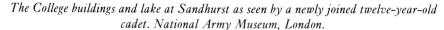

The College buildings and lake at Sandhurst as seen by a newly joined twelve-year-old cadet. National Army Museum, London.

using many thousands of trees. The area had been aptly described by William Cobbett in his *Rural Rides* as 'that sweep of barrenness which exhibits itself between the Golden Farmer Hill and Blackwater'. The Golden Farmer Inn stands at the top of the hill on the main London road down into Bagshot, and in these more prosaic days is named the Jolly Farmer. The site in those days, however, was a favourite haunt of a successful highwayman known as the 'Golden Farmer', who turned out to be the vicar of the nearby parish of Yateley. This remarkable cleric earned his sobriquet through 'dealing' only in golden sovereigns.

The area around the Sandhurst estate was not only sparsely wooded, it was also very thinly populated. Bagshot was a mere hamlet; Blackwater consisted only of a few poor cottages. Le Marchant, indeed, chose the site for the College 'as to avoid a neighbourhood injurious to the morals of the cadets and which allows space for military movements and the construction of military works without interruption'.

With the approval of Mr Wyatt's plans and the appointment of a contractor, a Mr Copeland who was engaged in building barracks in many parts of the country, the Lieutenant Governor must have felt that many of his problems were about to be resolved. Little could he have foreseen that nearly ten years would elapse before the college building at Sandhurst would be ready for even partial occupation.

HARCOURT, THE ABSENTEE GOVERNOR

With the resumption of the war with France, Le Marchant's friends at Horse Guards could spare little time to listen to his problems of inadequate housing at Marlow and shortage of staff. General Harcourt's appointment as Governor of the College had been a further setback. Dilatory, unbusinesslike and infirm, he refused to reside anywhere close to the College and spent most of the year at Brighton or St Leonards and other resorts as far away as Bath and Malvern Wells. His occasional visits to the College did little to relieve Le Marchant of the tedium of endless correspondence on minor matters about which he insisted on being kept informed. Feeling his own position to be a reward for past services, he was not prepared to exert himself in supporting the Lieutenant Governor's plans. In these attitudes Harcourt found an ally in the Commandant of the Junior Department, Lieutenant Colonel James Butler, an elderly gunner officer with no experience of active service. Between Butler's obstructive tactics and fierce independence, and Harcourt's studied indifference, Le Marchant found his authority undermined and all his future plans for the College endangered.

PLANS IN JEOPARDY

Meanwhile at Sandhurst Mr Copeland had set up temporary huts for his workmen and started to make bricks on site in order to save the cost of transportation. While the contractor was hedging on this initial outlay, as he still awaited formal authority to start building and suspected that the estimates would be cut back in any case, the Treasury were anxious to quash the whole idea of undertaking new construction work where existing buildings could be utilised, for the cost of the war was steadily mounting. But the demand for officers was also soaring and the scheme for taking the sons of serving officers at reduced fees was producing a flood applicants for the Junior Department of the RMC. In 1806, with some 300 cadets under training and a fourth company forming at Marlow, there were urgent demands for extra temporary accommodation. Seeking a cheaper solution, the Treasury pressed for the move of both departments into any State-owned building, almost regardless of its situation or condition. An empty hospital at Chatham, Nottingham Castle, the King's palace at Winchester, all in turn proved too small or too expensive to adapt, so to Le Marchant's great relief these alternatives were dropped.

In the meantime the prospects of ever building on the Sandhurst site seemed even more remote than before. The great piles of bricks, hastily made years before, had proved to be worthless. For months all seemed in the balance, until a change of government brought Lord Castlereagh back as Minister of War. Here was a minister who was pressing to raise the strength of the land forces to over a million, whose plans included setting up an Army school 'where boys could pass two or three years in education' before joining a regiment on a seven-year engagement, whose interest in a national college for officers went beyond vague promises.

THE TREASURY WON OVER

In May 1808 the Supreme Board of the College submitted a strong recommendation to the Treasury in favour of the Sandhurst site, pointing out the urgency of the matter – that it was seven years since the land had been purchased and a contractor appointed. The document specified the essential establishment for the College headquarters and the Junior Department of 412 cadets, and underlined three carefully framed arguments. Firstly the point was made that in proposing a building to house only one department there would be a saving on the original estimate. Similarly there would be no need to rent the 'temporary and inadequate accommodation, obtained at considerable expense in the town of Marlow'. Finally, to remove 'the objection of there being no town in the immediate vicinity of Sandhurst where the professors and masters can be lodged', it

Cadets of the Junior Department RMC in 1813. RMA Sandhurst Collection.

was pointed out that the contractor had agreed to build houses at his own expense and recover the cost through charging rent.

The reaction of the Treasury officials on reading these proposals can well be imagined! Not only could they save money on the original cost of the building, but they would also be saving all the rents at Marlow, and by building a few cheap houses they could themselves collect rents from the unfortunate professors who would have nowhere else to live. Within six months Treasury approval was given for work to start immediately on the college building at Sandhurst at a revised estimate of £89,770, it being agreed that other necessary work could be considered later. So, after years of delay and at the very start of the Peninsular War, Le Marchant's plans for a permanent home for the Royal Military College were brought to fruition, albeit at a cut price and in truncated form, as the Senior Department was not to move. But of all those involved it was perhaps only James Wyatt who had any inkling of the final cost of building Sandhurst.

CHAPTER 3

Building for Posterity

A TIME TO EXPAND

The inadequacy of the accommodation for the Royal Military Academy at Woolwich had been obvious for some time. Back in 1783, when the cadets were sleeping five in a room and the classrooms were equally overcrowded, a possible move to a large private house and estate at Blackheath had been debated in the House of Commons and the project referred to the Committee of Supply. But nothing had come of it, and by the turn of the century the cadet barracks were in such a state of disrepair that it was decided that they must be rebuilt. However, the renewal of the war with France, after the 1802 Peace of Amiens, called for an increase in the establishment of the Cadet Company to 100, and the request came for up to forty extra places for cadets for the East India Company.

Unlike the newly formed RMC, the Academy had been officially recognised for many years and few would have disputed that its maintenance from public funds was in the national interest. Indeed, with the annual estimate for 1799 set at £3,150, in a year when costs had risen sharply and it was full to overflowing, the Academy was being run at a very low cost. So when the Master General of the Ordnance, John, second Earl of Chatham, decided to have a new home for the Academy built on Woolwich Common there was no delay in voting the necessary funds. The task of designing the building was given to James Wyatt, but as we shall see later he was allowed little or no margin to cater for any increase in the strength of the Cadet Company.

Leaving aside the problems caused by overcrowding, the war years had been difficult ones for the Academy staff at Woolwich. The urgent demands for more and more young officers to be commissioned had meant that the course of studies had been completely disorganised and standards had fallen progressively. The practice of holding public examinations had been abandoned almost immediately and Lieutenant Colonel Twiss, the Lieutenant Governor, was not able to recommend their reintroduction until 1802, nine years later. Within a few months the country was again at war, and over the next twelve months sixty-seven cadets were called forward for commissioning. Of these only one was accepted for the Engineers, none of the others being considered sufficiently qualified. The demand was such, however, that a few of the more advanced students were appointed Assistant Engineers and sent abroad with the chance of earning their commissions in the field.

In February of the same year the Master General came to an agreement with General Harcourt that cadets who had qualified for entrance to the Academy and were waiting for vacancies should start their training at Marlow. These were known as 'Ordnance cadets', and the establishment of the Academy was adjusted accordingly. To provide for commissioning 40 gentlemen cadets a year as Artillery or Engineer officers, there should be 100 cadets at Woolwich, and 60 Ordnance cadets, plus up to 20 East India cadets, at Marlow, and a further 10 extra cadets studying at private schools.

NEW BUILDINGS ON THE COMMON

By the time the new accommodation on Woolwich Common was ready for occupation in 1806 the number of cadets under instruction had been pushed up again. Wyatt's fine buildings now proved too small to take any but the 128 of the senior class, known as the Higher Establishment, while the remaining 180 had to be split between part of the old barracks in the Royal Arsenal and Marlow. To mention just one of the problems that arose from this situation, we find the Lieutenant Governor asking that the Inspector and one of the captains be 'allowed forage for one horse each, as they have occasion to visit both the Departments of the Institution repeatedly in one day'. The Board's reply was 'that they cannot, consistently with the regulations, comply with the suggestion'.

The new buildings for the Academy, whilst inadequate to house the full wartime numbers, provided greatly improved living and working conditions. Each of the four divisions was separately housed and had its own classroom. In addition there was a library, a large lecture room and two model rooms for general use. The provision of a fencing room and two racquet courts at least recognised the recreational needs of young men who were often cooped up for long hours at their studies. Within the area enclosed by the rectangle of buildings were a number of courts or parade grounds, one for each division, and a larger, centrally placed, assembly area; otherwise the space was walled off as gardens which were allocated for the use of the officers on the staff and the housekeeper.

While the general layout could give an impression of spaciousness, with a strong emphasis on improving academic facilities, the intention to

33

regiment and control the cadets was equally evident. The officers' quarters were built in line with and directly connected to those occupied by the cadets, while each wing of two divisions, with officers' quarters sandwiched in the middle, formed a compact and readily supervised 'command' for one of the captains. The Lieutenant Governor, both Inspectors and the senior professor, Issac Landemann, the Professor of Fortification, were all provided with houses outside the Academy precincts. The remaining professors and masters, as before, had to find their own accommodation.

In outline, the staff in 1810 consisted of the Lieutenant Governor, two captains and four subalterns, together with a chaplain, a surgeon and a quartermaster. On the educational staff there was an Inspector and an Assistant Inspector, both serving officers, and the following professors and masters: for fortification, three; mathematics, eight; drawing, four; French, two; and chemistry, one. In addition there was a dancing master and a fencing instructor and two modellers. A warrant officer assisted the quartermaster and there were two clerks. Two housekeepers were employed (one at the Royal Arsenal barracks), a hospital nurse, sixteen servants, a porter and four sweepers.

LINKS WITH MARLOW

Soon after the move had taken place Lieutenant Colonel Butler, probably at the insistence of Le Marchant, asked to be informed of the duties of the housekeeper at Woolwich and the meals she provided. The reply sent

The new buildings for the Royal Military Academy on Woolwich Common, c. 1810.
RMA Sandhurst Collection.

to Marlow stated that the diet was bread and milk for breakfast and bread and cheese for supper. For dinner each cadet had about a pound of beef or mutton with potatoes or greens, and one day a week fruit pies or rice pudding. The housekeeper, normally an officer's widow, received no salary but instead 1*s.* 1*d.* a day for each cadet. This had to cover full board, the cook's wages and the provision of table linen. At the new Academy on the Common twenty-four cauldrons of coal were allowed annually for cooking for 128 cadets. A proportionate quantity was allowed for the sixty cadets at the Lower Barracks, who had a housekeeper of their own.

The question of the uniform to be worn by the Ordnance cadets at Marlow was also the subject of correspondence as the Master General of Ordnance suggested that, on grounds of economy, their uniform should be the same as the one they would later wear at Woolwich. In 1810 any disagreements about this were resolved by the decision of the East India Company to open their own military college at Addiscombe. The removal of their cadets from Woolwich now made room for the Ordnance cadets to be gradually withdrawn from Marlow. Two years later, in the winter of 1812–13, the Junior Department of the Royal Military College moved to Sandhurst.

Le Marchant's Plans Supported

The decision to build at Sandhurst was a triumph for Le Marchant and reflected the high regard in which he was held by many influential officers at Horse Guards and by the King himself. Le Marchant's son Denis, when a schoolboy at Eton, had once accompanied his father to an audience at Windsor. Later Denis recalled the words spoken by the King one evening on the terrace at Windsor: 'I consider the Military College an object of the deepest national importance . . . you will all the time be raising a race of officers, who will make our army the finest in Europe. The country is greatly indebted to you.' This was high praise indeed and well earned, for few outside his family and close associates knew of the pressures and multitudinous calls on Le Marchant's time and energy, and over all the need to exercise iron self-control, so contrary to his nature, when facing his critics and detractors. In 1808 his perseverance brought more than the decision to build at Sandhurst. A new and very detailed royal warrant was published, supporting virtually all of his earlier proposals as to the organisation, staffing and courses for both departments.

Four companies would be carried on the establishment of the Army and the gentlemen cadets would be paid 2s. 6d. a day. This sum was to be applied to their instruction, clothing and maintenance and would not be in diminution of any fees paid. The warrant made it clear that any cadets who acquired a commission 'during their continuance at the College, not in

Interior of a barrack room at the RMA, showing various dress worn in 1810–12.
Records of the RMA.

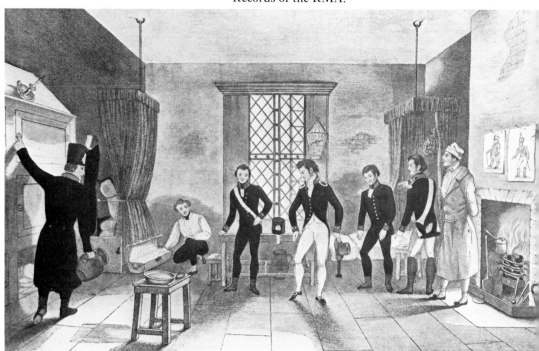

consequence of their progress in their studies, shall still be amenable to all the rules and regulations'. On the other hand, any who displayed 'a superior capacity and application' would be given the time and opportunity to acquire 'a perfect military education'. On qualifying for a commission and being recommended by the Governor they should be granted the brevet rank of ensign and be permitted 'to remain at the College and still persevere in their studies'. All fees would be waived, and providing they reached the standards laid down for the course and were equal to the duties of a lieutenant, they would be commissioned in that rank without purchase in one of the line regiments of the Cavalry or Infantry. This, indeed, had been one of Le Marchant's objectives and there is little doubt that it and many more of the regulations were inspired and probably drafted by him personally.

Much activity now centred on the Sandhurst estate, where the digging of the foundations of the building had at last been started. With the renewal of hostilities and the departure of many regiments overseas, there was indeed a pervading air of urgency. Applications for places at Marlow had increased to the point at which special regulations had to be brought in, requiring that the candidates must be at least 4 foot 9 inches (145 cm) tall and thirteen years old, and by 1809 there were 320 cadets under instruction.

Tea Caddy Row

At Sandhurst there was still much to be arranged. There were the complicated legal negotiations, eventually requiring an Act of Parliament, to divert the road from Sandhurst village that ran past the mill and on towards Bagshot so that it did not pass straight in front of the College building. But the first priority was to complete the negotiations with Mr Parfitt for the purchase of his two fields that lay below the mill and next to the London Road, for this was where the professors' houses were to be built and the contract with the builder must be agreed with the Treasury before they had second thoughts.

The contracts decided upon were for £1,310 for the land and £42,258 for the construction of thirteen double houses. All were to the same design but each of the four professors would be allotted a complete 'double' house, while the eighteen junior masters and their families would each have to put up with a semi-detached house and half the accommodation. Dubbed 'Tea Caddy Row' by the coachmen who plied the road to Bath, these 'professors' houses' in cheap yellow brick, standing square, regimented and unadorned, still remind us of Le Marchant's active concern for those of his staff whose responsibility it was to 'ground the cadets in science'.

A True Memorial

During the early summer of 1811 the Lieutenant Governor rode over to Sandhurst with his son Denis on one of his regular visits to see the progress of the work. Turning to his son, Le Marchant remarked that he felt that his struggles to get the College on a proper footing would now be at an end and that it was here at Sandhurst that he could expect to 'pass the remainder of his days [and] witness the accomplishment of the schemes that had occupied him for so many years'. But the Fates had decided otherwise. Within days his promotion to Major General was notified, and with it an intimation that the Commander-in-Chief could not agree to his remaining in his present appointment, which was incompatible with the higher rank.

The real reason for Le Marchant's removal from the College soon emerged. John Gaspard Le Marchant, the 'Scientific Soldier' whom many regarded as the finest leader of cavalry in the Service, was to proceed immediately to join Lord Wellington in Spain where he would take command of the newly formed Heavy Cavalry Brigade. Almost exactly a year later the General was killed at Salamanca in the dying moments of the battle in which he had led his brigade in a series of charges that broke the French centre, putting the seal to one of Wellington's most brilliant victories – in the words of the historian Sir Charles Oman, 'the defeat of 40,000 Frenchman in 40 minutes'. His country's gratitude was marked by valedictory speeches in both Houses of Parliament, a state pension to provide for his orphan children and a memorial in St Paul's Cathedral. But his true memorial lay in the hearts of the men he had led and of the 1,700 student officers and cadets who had passed through his hands while he was Lieutenant Governor of the College that owed its very existence to his inspiration and dedicated efforts.

A New Governor

General Harcourt's retirement conveniently took place in June 1811 and Major General Sir Alexander Hope, KB, arrived immediately as the new Governor. Sir Alexander had long been associated with the affairs of the College, as in 1799, at the exceptionally early age of thirty, he had been Deputy Adjutant General and played an important part in setting up the Senior Department at High Wycombe. Unlike Harcourt, who had consistently refused to live anywhere near the College, the new Governor had already decided to occupy the manor house when the cadets moved to Sandhurst. Meanwhile Colonel Howard Douglas was recalled from Spain as Commandant of the Senior Department, which now moved nearer to Sandhurst. A house in West Street, Farnham, later known as College

Gardens, had been purchased and, after extensive repairs and alterations, became the new home of the Senior Department from 1814 for the next seven years. As for filling the post of Lieutenant Governor, it seems that no one could think of a suitable reason for not promoting Butler.

EARLY DAYS AT SANDHURST

For the first twelve months or so after the cadets moved to Sandhurst the conditions must have been difficult for everyone. The main building was far from being finished and work on the creation of training facilities such as fieldworks had not even been started. With construction work going on in various parts of the grounds, there were workmen and soldiers everywhere. The latter were working parties from a nearby Militia regiment who were being kept busy digging out the mill stream and pond to form the lower lake. The soil was then being used to level a parade ground, known as the 'exercise ground', in front of the College building. The contractor's accounts show that some 3,500 loads of earth were shifted in local carts hired at 6*d.* a load.

It is often argued that the building-up of what is now Old College Parade Ground was carried out in this way to 'cover up' or screen the basement, so as to improve the elevation of the building as a whole, and that this theory is borne out by the submission of supplementary estimates of £4,800 for the 'front area and pedestal to the College and house of paymaster and surgeon'. It is, however, far more likely that Wyatt never changed the original plans he had drawn up. Having placed the front of the building on a low ridge, he had then dug down for sound foundations, always intending that the basement should be *sous-sol*, and that funds would be found to finish off the brickwork for the area and fence wall later. In fact a further supplementary estimate provided for continuing the fence wall to join up with the houses built for the paymaster and the surgeon away on the flanks of the main building. This time Wyatt nearly overplayed his hand as the cost of this particular embellishment, slipped in alongside a proposal to erect *chevaux de frise* to open to the public the best view of the College along 600 feet (183 metres) of the Great Western Road, amounted to £3,700.

As Lieutenant Colonel Mockler-Ferryman writes in *Annals of Sandhurst*, 'the war had made the Army popular with the nation, and Sandhurst was training officers for the Army; expense was nothing, and so long as the money was forthcoming, it was readily spent'. One item purchased in 1813 is of especial interest – an organ for the chapel costing £500 – for this was the year of a very important occasion, the Presentation of Colours to the Royal Military College.

The date chosen for the ceremony was 12 September 1813, and a few days previously the tone was set by the publication of an order: 'The captains will send a return to the Lieutenant Governor's office . . . of any articles of clothing required to complete any cadet . . . in order that every one may appear in the most perfect state before Her Majesty.' In the morning Queen Charlotte drove over from Windsor, accompanied by the Prince Regent, the Commander-in-Chief the Duke of York, the Duke of Cambridge, the Prince of Orange and the Duke of Brunswick.

HM Queen Charlotte presenting Colours to the RMC in 1813. No. XI in James Mudie's *Series of National Medals, issued in 1820. Crookshank Collection, RMA Sandhurst.*

After the royal party had been received by the cadet battalion Her Majesty took up her position on the steps of the Grand Entrance, being joined by the Prince Regent and the Commander-in-Chief. This was the signal for the Colours to be brought from the Chapel (now the Indian Army Memorial Room) and carried out to the portico by Colonel Butler and Sir Howard Douglas, who delivered them to the two royal princes standing on either side of the Queen. Before presenting the Colours Her Majesty, in a short speech, paid tribute to all those whose efforts had resulted in 'making this noble provision for the instruction of young officers, and for the early education of those destined for the military service'. The Colours were then received by the Governor, who in turn handed them to the two cadets appointed as colour-bearers. The whole assembly then moved into the Chapel. The Colours having been placed on the altar, the service of the day was read by the Chaplain and the Colours were consecrated.

The words carried on the Regimental Colour were '*Vires acquirit eundo*', which remained the motto of the College for the whole of its separate existence. This phrase from Virgil's *Aeneid* calling for a progressive 'gathering of strength' had, as Her Majesty pointed out, wide implications – particularly for those cadets who, with an 'honest ambition', were struggling to pass their examinations!

After the service the Queen visited the dining rooms, where according to a report in the *Star* 'her entry was the signal for saying grace and beginning the meal'. Next Her Majesty inspected the hospital, 'where however there were no sick – a proof of the salubrity of the situation'; or more likely the foresight of the Surgeon. 'The royal party then moved to Government House to dine. Here, having done credit to the hospitality of the worthy Governor and his very amiable lady, they enjoyed the amusement of dancing in the evening.'

FINANCE AND NUMBERS CUT

So long as the Napoleonic War lasted and there was the urgent demand for officers the Treasury continued to take a sympathetic view of Sir Alexander Hope's requests, both for a completion of the buildings and an improvement in the facilities at Sandhurst. In 1813 the call for officers had been so great that cadets of the first two departments (orphans and the sons of junior officers), who still needed to pass their final exams, were allowed to join the Army as volunteers with the rank and pay of ensigns. Furthermore they received a free uniform allowance of £57. 4s. 10d. Their places at the College were quickly filled and it was only in 1824 that the number of companies was reduced to three. By this time, however, the Treasury had tightened the screw and the College faced severe financial restrictions.

Outstanding construction work around the estate was completed towards the end of 1817. Wyatt's final accounts were then presented, and the total for the buildings and the fencing and other work on the estate came to a few pounds short of £370,000.

At about this date the Governor raised the question of instruction in equitation. Properly set up with stabling, an indoor school and quarters for the staff, the cost would be £12,500, plus an annual grant of £1,400. This request was in line with one of Le Marchant's original proposals, that cadets intended for the Cavalry should have such facilities; but it was four or five years before a grant of £6,000 was promised to build a 'riding house', which in fact was not completed until 1825. In the meantime some very temporary stabling, formerly used by the Wagon Train (later to become the Royal Army Service Corps), was taken over. Eventually a troop sergeant major, three roughriders and a few private soldiers arrived with twenty horses. Under these conditions, however, and until the indoor school was built, the riding establishment only operated during the summer months.

Training facilities were not the only items of expenditure that were cut back. At the very moment that the contractor's men were putting the last touches to the College building the Treasury announced the first round of 'inevitable' economies that would mark the successful ending of the war. Starting at the top, the Governor was to lose his 'table-money'. This was a special entertainment allowance which had been granted in 1814 to help cover the expenses of running Government House, expenses that in the High Wycombe days Harcourt had been careful to avoid and Le Marchant had been forced to meet as best as he could out of his own pocket. Next, the Commandants of both departments were required to give up part of their pay and allowances to the tune of £714 a year. The number of professors and masters was reduced by six, and those that remained were required to work longer hours. These and other savings, which included stopping the messing grant for the student officers living at Farnham and cutting expenditure on the cadets' food, totalled over £6,000 annually.

Lake House and the Fort on Flagstaff Hill in 1830. From a sketch by Gentleman Cadet Austin.

The savings, however, were not considered enough. Later in the year the Treasury conceived the plan of manipulating the scale of fees paid for the three categories of cadets. The number of places for orphans was cut to 80, raising to 130 the places for the sons of serving officers, who paid according to rank, and finally the fees for the remainder were increased to £126 a year. Assuming the latter numbered 120, this would produce a further credit of £4,000 a year. As a sop to the 'nobility and gentry', who would be paying the top fees for their sons' education, it was announced that astronomy and natural philosophy would be added to the curriculum.

EDUCATIONAL STANDARDS REVISED

At this point the Governor began to look ahead to the establishment of cadets being further reduced and the situation where the entry standard must be adjusted accordingly. Drawing attention to the fact that many applicants for admission 'from want of education in childhood either failed to enter, or are rejected after the probationary year', he proposed changes in the entrance examination and raising the standards for commissioning. These proposals were adopted, and shortly afterwards Sir Alexander Hope left to be Governor of Edinburgh Castle, handing over at Sandhurst to Major General Sir George Murray, GCB, a former Quartermaster General under Lord Wellington.

With the Treasury still pressing for economies, General Murray decided that a reorganisation of the Senior Department might meet their demands and at the same time be of benefit to the Service. He proposed closing Farnham completely. With fewer cadets, the students could now be accommodated at Sandhurst, where, with only two extra instructors, there would be sufficient staff for both departments. This would not only bring the whole College under one roof, as had always been intended, but would result in a saving of over £5,000 in pay and allowances. The plan was readily endorsed and the following year (1821) the student officers moved into part of the Terrace, with an overflow lodging in York Town. Sir Howard Douglas, who was now out of a job, received an allowance pending another appointment; but there is no record that the masters who were 'removed' when Farnham closed down received similar treatment.

MORE LEAN YEARS

Over the next ten years the downward slide continued. The orphan class was abolished except for ten cadet scholarships awarded by the Commander-in-Chief. The cadet establishment fell to 180, organised in two companies. The appointment of Major and Superintendent of Studies was abolished, and a further reduction of two captains and seven masters was ordered. Finally, in 1832, the Parliamentary Vote (the annual grant from public funds) was abruptly withdrawn. From now on and until public opinion was roused to the plight of the Services during the Crimean War, nearly a quarter of a century later, the College had to be self-supporting.

During these lean and critical years all now depended on the efforts and loyalty of a handful of dedicated officers and professors. Here mention must be made of those who bore the responsibility for the management of the College, General Sir E. Paget, GCB, the Governor from 1826 to 1836, and General Sir George Scovell, KCB, Lieutenant Governor from 1830 to 1836, who carried on as Governor until 1855. Both had served with distinction under the Duke of Wellington, who took a very active interest in their stewardship of the Royal Military College. 'The Duke's Day', when the Commander-in-Chief inspected the cadets and presided over the Board of Commissioners, became a highlight in the Sandhurst year, corresponding in many ways to the Sovereign's Parade of modern times. Nor was the Duke less attentive to the status of the College in his nominations to the Board of Commissioners. In 1846, for instance, in addition to the Secretary for War and two royal Field Marshals, fifteen high-ranking officers of wide experience and considerable distinction served on the Board and over half of these were full generals, including several former Governors of the College.

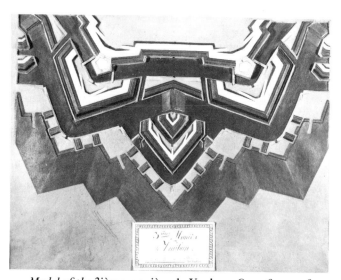

Model of the 3ième manière de Vauban. *One of a set of models used for instruction in fortification and presented by Sir Howard Douglas. RMA Sandhurst Collection.*

CHAPTER 4

Royal Visits and Pitched Battles

ROYALTY AT WOOLWICH

Shortly after the armistice with France in the spring of 1814 there was an important royal visit to the Royal Military Academy. The inspecting officer was HRH The Prince Regent, who was accompanied by the Emperor of Russia, the King of Prussia, the Duke of York, the Master General the Earl of Mulgrave, and Generals Blücher, de Yorck, Bülow and Count Platov. On arrival the visitors were met by a Royal Salute fired from light three-pounders. This was followed by the inspection of the Guard of Honour, who then gave a display of arms drill by performing the manual exercise.

After inspecting the barrack rooms, library and model room, and the various classes at work, the royal party breakfasted in the cadet dining room. The cadets dined in the racquet court and were allowed half a pint of port with which to drink the royal toasts. Thus fortified, the guard again paraded to pay appropriate compliments to the visitors on departure. All went off most satisfactorily. The Prince Regent expressed his 'perfect satisfaction', and the Emperor requested that the cadets should be 'permitted to rest from their studies' on the following day.

A SHORTAGE OF COMMISSIONS

In the same year the Lieutenant Governor, Colonel Mudge, became increasingly concerned over the Master General's policy of not filling vacant commissions, in anticipation of the strength of the Army being drastically reduced under peacetime conditions. He pointed out that the average age of the twenty-nine cadets in the first class was over nineteen and that many of them had spent over four years at the Academy. He understood that there were currently some forty vacancies in the Artillery and twenty-eight in the Engineers. While he realised that little could be done when there were so many officers on half-pay, he asked if twelve of the class could now be commissioned 'so as to keep up emulation in the studies' at the Academy.

As a special concession the best nine cadets were commissioned, but over the next few years the situation worsened. The number of cadets under instruction was progressively reduced by limiting the entries, and the age of those in the top class continued to rise, an extreme example being that of a cadet who spent eight years at the Academy. In 1819 the number of cadets was down to 150, but their prospects of obtaining commissions within a reasonable period of time were no better.

The maintenance of discipline now became increasingly difficult. Matters were brought to a head when a cadet in the third class, who refused to sign an agreement drawn up by his less industrious classmates to cut down on his work, was subjected to what was officially described as a 'violent outrage'. This beating-up was of such a serious nature that the matter was referred to the Master General. It happened that the Duke of Wellington had just taken over the appointment, and the miscreants received very short shrift indeed. Eleven cadets were summarily dismissed and a further ten relegated to the bottom class, while the two corporals most concerned were stripped of all ranks and privileges.

Shortly afterwards Colonel Mudge died, and his successor, Colonel Ford, continued to agitate about vacancies for first commissions. He argued that under existing conditions, and until the half-pay list was run out, the situation could arise where a cadet joining at the age of fifteen might not be commissioned until he was over twenty-four years old and then be placed immediately on half-pay! With his customary direct approach the Duke issued the following orders. The establishment of cadets was to be gradually reduced to 100 by accepting only one applicant for every two vacancies. Any cadet who reached the age of twenty, or had been five years at the Academy without qualifying for a commission by public examination, would be dismissed. Those who qualified for a commission within these limitations of age and attendance would be transferred to the Royal Arsenal for an advanced course in laboratory work and other practical subjects, on the successful completion of which they would be sent home on cadet pay to await commissioning as vacancies occurred. Meanwhile all cadets should be accommodated in the Upper Academy, i.e. the new buildings on the Common.

As a result of these decisions Colonel Ford faced the unenviable task of not only removing a number of the older cadets, but also dismissing the staff involved with the practical class living in the Warren, together with five masters. Over the next three years we find that sixteen cadets received commissions and a further fifty-three qualified and passed through the course at the Arsenal before being 'returned to their friends'. Twenty of these latter, however, soon found themselves ordered to Ireland where they were required to assist in carrying out the Trigonometric Survey.

With the ending of the Napoleonic War no less than 220,000 men, including 80,000 militia, were discharged, and by 1822 the Regular Army had been reduced to 100,000, all ranks. At this date the Artillery and Engineers mustered around 7,000 (the proportion being six to one), compared with 30,000 at the height of the war. Year by year Parliament had been trimming the numbers and cutting the Service Estimates, and this policy indeed continued, but before the end of the decade Parliament's hand had been forced. Caught unprepared and with inadequate forces to cover emergencies, such as the situations in Ireland and in the West Indies and the war in Burma, to name but some of the crises, let alone the unrest at home, the Government had to act. The establishment of the Line Regiments was restored by raising the number of companies from eight to ten, and additional battalions were raised for service overseas.

The first demand for more officers came around 1825, by which date the establishment of the Cadet Company at Woolwich had been officially set at sixty. In this year forty-five gentlemen cadets were commissioned into Line Regiments, seventeen into the Artillery and five into the Engineers. Many of these were aged twenty-three and had been sent home after qualifying, but there were still sixty in this category waiting for vacancies. Over the next ten years the prospects for the Woolwich cadets gradually improved and we find that in the early 1830s there was an average of 125 under instruction with an annual intake of about 36, while the number receiving commissions each year averaged 24 at the age of a little over eighteen. Prospects of promotion were poor, to say the least. For instance, one captain of the Royal Artillery, who had taken part in every battle in the Peninsular War, was still serving in that rank in 1836, and the average term of service required at this date to reach the rank of first (or senior) captain was forty years.

A QUESTION OF FEES

As a result of a reorganisation of the Ordnance Department's finances it was decided in 1831 to charge the parents fees for their sons' education at Woolwich. The scale ranged from £80 a year for the sons of noblemen and private gentlemen down to £20 for orphans. This was a good deal less than at Sandhurst, where the top rate was £125 and where in 1835 the fees for the sons of junior officers, including orphans, were £40 a year. From this date and for many years to come both establishments were required to be self-supporting, as the Governor of the RMC, Lieutenant General Sir E. Paget, KCB, was told that the Government grant was being withdrawn.

By 1837, when Major General Sir George Scovell, KCB, took over as

Governor, the College accounts could no longer be balanced and there was a deficit of £1,700 to be reported to the Treasury. The Government responded by proposing that the few remaining free places, those in the gift of the Commander-in-Chief, should be reduced on the grounds that 'it is doubtful if it is desirable in time of peace to introduce into the Army officers without means'. Subsequent correspondence on the subject went rather further and contained a denial that it was intended to suppress the College, but stressed that matters must in the future be so arranged that it was completely self-supporting. Stung by these words, the Governor pointed out that his predecessor had struggled towards this end under considerable difficulties; that the Terrace houses had been neither repainted nor repaired for twenty years; that Government House itself was (metaphorically) falling down; and that if he was expected to finance the College himself, this could only be achieved by increasing the number of cadets, reducing the staff and clamping down on such essentials as repairing the field fortification works. An increase of ten cadets was agreed and briefly allowed to be implemented, but it was soon cancelled, bringing the establishment back to 180.

Only the disasters in the Crimea brought a change in Government policy and the restoration of a grant in aid. The truth was that owing to the purchase system the majority of young men commissioned into the Cavalry or Infantry had never been near Sandhurst. Many commanding officers, indeed, preferred to take 'purchase' officers into their regiments, a policy which was encouraged by those senior officers who themselves owed their high rank and position to the system of buying and selling of commissions that had become so deeply embedded. The situation is well illustrated by some statistics given by Gwyn Harries-Jenkins in *The Army in Victorian Society*.

First Commissions granted in the Army: 1834–38

Regiments	Commissions by purchase	Commissions by non-purchase	Total
Cavalry	221	6	227
Guards	34	8	42
Line	859	246	1,105
TOTAL	1,114	260	1,374
From the Ranks	3	33	36
TOTAL	1,117	293	1,410

Inspection Day, 1805. The Junior Department of the Royal Military College parading at Marlow for the Annual Inspection. RMA Sandhurst Collection.

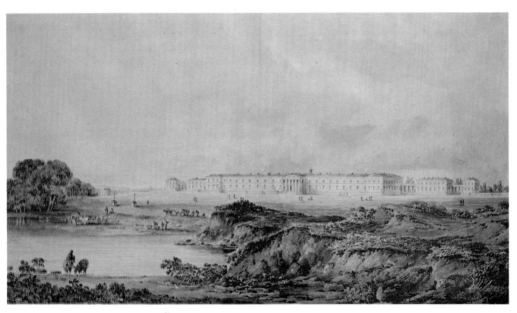

The Sandhurst site, c. 1811, showing the progress on the College buildings and work on digging out the lake. RMA Sandhurst Collection.

The arrival of HM King William IV to present Colours to the RMC in 1835.
RMA Sandhurst Collection.

The Terrace or 'Tea Caddy Row', a view from the York Town Gate.
RMA Sandhurst Collection.

RMA Course Improved

At Woolwich the situation was rather different. Here the opportunities were better, the numbers were rising, and the fees were lower. Furthermore the system of education was steadily being improved, certainly to a greater extent than was possible at Sandhurst. Credit for this must go to the personal influence of Sir George Murray, who filled the appointment of Master General of the Ordnance from 1834 to 1835 and again from 1841 to 1846. Soon after first being appointed he set up a committee to examine the work of the Academy. The result was a raising of the entrance standard through the institution of a competitive examination. Apart from the usual tests in English, mathematics and classics, the other 'indispensable' subjects were French, geography, history and elementary drawing, while preference was to be given to candidates who could show progress in Greek and German.

As for the syllabus of the course at Woolwich, the study of German was introduced, together with lectures on history and geography, while more emphasis was to be placed on plan-drawing and surveying. To achieve this, extra staff were to be added on the academic side, namely six civilian masters and two officers. The latter would receive 5s. a day in addition to their pay, one officer being specially employed to teach history and geography. The hours of study were to be increased to eight in summer and seven in winter, and to teach the extra number of cadets most of the masters would be required to put in more attendances. Only the Professor of Mathematics, the French master and the drawing master, however, would get any compensatory allowance.

More Royal Visits

Royal visits to the cadet establishments in the last century were rather less frequent than they are nowadays. From time to time there were royal visits to Woolwich, but these were strictly Gunner occasions, with the Cadet Company parading with the rest of the garrison. At a review of the Royal Artillery held soon after his accession King William IV noticed the cadets drawn up on the right of the Foot Artillery and asked who had ordered them out on parade. 'On being told that "the Commandant of the Garrison had give the order", he said that no one had the authority to order out the Cadet Company but himself, and the Brigade Major was immediately sent to direct the gentlemen cadets to return to their barracks.'

The first visit to either of the cadet establishments by a sovereign was made by King William IV to the Royal Military College in the autumn of 1835. An engraving recording the scene on the arrival of Their Majesties, by William Delamotte, the Professor of Landscape Drawing, gives many

Left *Uniforms at the Shop in 1844. On the left, full dress. The other cadet wears undress uniform, with a chevron on his arm for good conduct, while gold lace on the collar shows he has received a prize for proficiency in study.* Records of the RMA.

Right *Grand Lodge, the main gateway to the Royal Military College, in 1848. From a sketch by Gentleman Cadet B. Gale.*

interesting details. According to a copy of the draft orders, the battalion was to be formed in a hollow square, with the guard of honour taking up the fourth side, within which the ceremony would take place.

The visit had been postponed from the previous year and in view of the amount of public interest that it had aroused locally General Paget decided to rearrange the parade so that the large assembly of spectators could have a better view of their Sovereign and of the full ceremonial of the occasion; on the day the battalion was therefore drawn up in line facing the lake. After the royal party had been met by a Royal Salute and the New Colours had been presented the Old Colours were to be handed to an officer nominated by the Governor. This would most probably have been Colonel Scovell, who as the Lieutenant Governor was most directly concerned with the cadet battalion. The Old Colours would then have become his personal property as the custom of laying up Colours in a cathedral or church had not then been adopted.

After the march-past Their Majesties were to be ushered to the Board Room to witness the examination of those gentlemen cadets who were recommended for commissions. This was to be followed by the award of honorary certificates to officers of the Senior Department who had qualified at a public examination held on the previous day. Those cadets who had satisfied the Examining Board would then be brought foward and

recommended to the royal favour for commissions. According to the draft orders, one hour was allotted for the parade and two hours for the examination and award of certificates. A short visit to the riding school followed, after which the royal party adjourned to the Board Room before dining in one of the cadet mess rooms.

It is uncertain whether this programme was adhered to in detail but the royal visit was a great success, and the parade was witnessed by practically the whole local population for miles around, the main contingent coming from Bagshot, the nearest village. On the departure of the royal party the cadets, bursting with loyalty, called for an encore to 'God Save the King'. Some of the onlookers being a little slow in removing their hats, had them knocked off. This caused an uproar and an immediate challenge to the excited cadets from some of the worthy inhabitants of Bagshot that they should fight it out on their home ground. A few afternoons later some fifty or sixty cadets armed with hockey sticks marched on the village.

The inhabitants, at first too few to resist, soon collected in numbers. Sticks, guns and other weapons were called into requisition, and the cadets saw that it was time to fall back on their base of operations. Sending the younger ones home, they covered their retreat and fought their way back, reaching the College in a somewhat battered and dishevelled condition, but in time for the last study of the day.

At this date the regulations for the Junior Department laid down that 'the period allowed to complete a young gentleman's education is four years. But, when a gentleman cadet has completed his eighteenth year, he can no longer remain at the College, without a special permission to that effect.' There were two terms each year of nineteen or twenty weeks' duration, divided by a six-week summer and a seven-week winter vacation. The daily routine was virtually unchanged since the Marlow days. Within a half-hour of 'rouse' being sounded the cadets were paraded for inspection. They were then marched to the Chapel for a short service which was followed by breakfast. Studies started at 8.30 a.m. and continued, except for an hour's drill in the middle of the morning, until dinner, which was at 2 p.m. By about 4.30 p.m. the cadets were back in their classrooms for another three or four hours' study, with a short break for supper. The cadets had to be in bed by 10 p.m. by which hour the doors of the College were locked.

There were no half-holidays, and the only concession on Saturday evening was the omission of the last period of study after supper. On Sundays there was always a church parade and after dinner the cadets were free to enjoy the rather limited recreational facilities that the College and its grounds could provide. In the summer there was cricket on the Governor's clover field, together with boating and swimming. In winter hockey was the most popular game, and skating when the lake was sufficiently frozen over. In bad weather, however, there was nothing but for the cadet to return to his dormitory and try to avoid being caught smoking or gambling. Some may have used the College library, but the stock of books was very limited and contained few if any novels and little else in the way of light reading.

By the middle of the century fives had been added to the games played at Sandhurst, one of the courts later being converted for racquets. As for organised physical training, the only mention in the records of the early period comes in the late 1820s, when the newly introduced Swedish gymnastic exercises were taught by a Swiss officer, Captain Clias. The experiment seems to have been short-lived, but the grassed area near the Governor's Gate continued to be known as 'Gimcracks'. This site was the traditional venue for the settling of disputes between cadets. As soon as the challenge was accepted the cry of 'Fit! Fit!' would go up and all within range would pour out of the building to form a ring. On the appearance of one of the sergeants, who turned out to see fair play, the two contestants would set to with bare fists. When both had had enough they would be marched to the hospital. Here a black draught would be administered to clear the blood and the winner and loser would be confined until their bruises had subsided. There were perhaps too few opportunities for the cadets to work off their natural high spirits. One of the highlights of 1861 was a pitched battle between two classes, led by their respective French professors, one of whom was a royalist and the other a republican.

BLACKWATER FAIR

An annual event of great importance to the cadets was the Blackwater Fair. This was held in November and was eagerly looked forward to. Being placed strictly out of bounds, its simple pleasures had all the attraction of the most exotic forbidden fruit. The fair was held in a small field opposite the White Hart public house. It was of some importance to the countryside on account of its market for cattle and horses. In the evening the local people flocked in, drawn by the music of the single merry-go-round, and the modest collection of sideshows and shooting galleries lit by innumerable flares. With plenty of drink consumed, there was generally a bit of excitement towards the end of the evening 'as the uniform and behaviour of the party from the College rubbed the civilian merrymakers up the wrong way; a free fight not infrequently wound up the entertainment,

'Sponging for Credits', a Woolwich Professor and his class in 1850. From a painting by G.B. Campion.

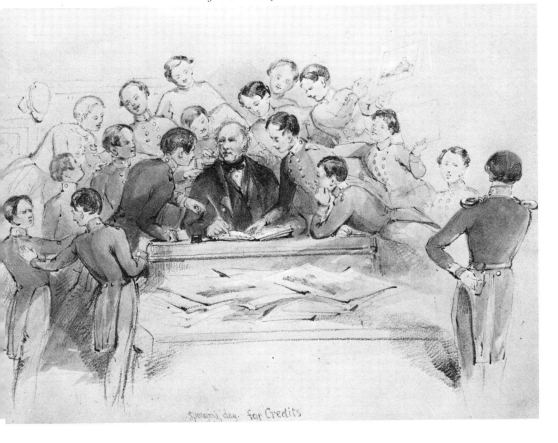

Sponging day for Credits

resulting in some prettily marked faces on parade the next morning and a long list of prisoners'.

For several years, around the early fifties, the date of the winter vacation was advanced, so as to avoid this annual brawling. The weakness of this somewhat feeble 'withdrawal' and the inconvenience of having to rearrange the terms eventually caused the decision to be reversed. Once again the fair was placed out of bounds, but proved even more popular with the cadets. Pickets of officers and staff sergeants were posted on the roads to Blackwater but were invariably evaded by a cross-country route and wading the river.

REGS AND JOHNS

During daylight hours a guard was mounted at the Grand Entrance. This was provided from the cadet companies, and those on duty were excused their studies for that particular day. The responsibility for maintaining discipline fell to the captains of the cadet companies, who seem to have been more or less permanently on call. In addition to turning out the guard at frequent intervals, and supervising the various parades and the attendance at classes, they were expected to be on constant watch for misconduct and 'crimes' of all kinds. These included baiting the masters and bullying the young and newly joined 'Johns' (derived from Johnny Raw – a young recruit), together with the more serious offences of being involved in the immoral practice of gambling or indulging in the antisocial and strictly forbidden habit of smoking. Frequent and unheralded visits were required to the dormitories, and a network of spies and informers, from amongst the college servants, had to be organised to cover the grounds and surrounding district, the latter being necessary to enforce the orders against cadets keeping horses or dogs and possessing firearms.

The cadets, who were accommodated on the upper floor of the building, slept five in a room. Each cadet had a large locker, which was screwed to the wall and known as a 'birdcage'. There was nowhere else for storing private possessions and contraband. The latter could vary from apples stolen from the Governor's garden to a complete smoking kit concealed in a cavity hollowed out in a large book, such as an innocent-looking Latin dictionary.

In spite of official disapproval and the efforts of the staff, the time-honoured system of 'fagging' continued under various guises, and the 'Johns' were usually willing to fag for the seniors, or 'Regs', to avoid mal-treatment. Consequently 'Johns' were regularly used as look-outs when a rag was in progress, or when the occupants of a room wished to indulge in smoking or playing cards. Smoking after lights out was usually conducted

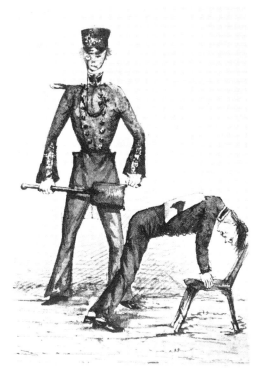

'Military Discipline' or
'Regs and Johns'. RMC
Record.

under the protection of a tent of blankets erected against the chimney breast. The blankets of course came from the John's bed.

Methods of persuading the juniors to smuggle contraband and co-operate generally with the wishes of their immediate superiors, the seniors, were ingenious and often painful. 'Shovelling' involved the John being spreadeagled on a table and beaten with racquets, bats and coal shovels. 'Ventilating' required that the recalcitrant cadet should be tied to one of the ventilators high up in the ceiling and then 'ventilated' with forks used as javelins. 'Adamising' was rather more subtle. The youthful victim was kidnapped after dark, taken secretly to a distant room on the other side of the building, stripped naked, and then lowered through a window to the ground. His only means of re-entry would then be through the guardroom. Here he must face and explain himself to that most terrifying and exalted being – the drill sergeant.

ON SURVIVAL
On Sandhurst, Charles Dickens comments (in *Dombey and Son*):

Major Bagstock did not recommend Mr Dombey to send his delicate Master Paul to the Royal Military College. None but the tough fellows could live through it at Sandhurst. We put each other to the torture there, we roasted the new fellows at a slow fire and hung 'em out of a three pair of stairs window with their heads downwards. I myself was held out of the window by the heels of my boots for thirteen minutes by the College clock.

It is unlikely that life for the cadets was much different from that in many boarding schools. The difference lay more in the degree of regimentation and discipline required in a military establishment and the fact that the age of entry for the cadets was gradually rising. The penalties for nonconformity and misbehaviour were, however, rather more severe.

For some time, and with only occasional small variations, the scale of punishment was as follows. For minor infringements of the rules, extra guards or drills and extra work were given, also confinement to the College grounds, which involved reporting to the guardroom at frequent intervals. Next, there was close or open arrest; a refinement of the latter required that the cadet be marched out of the mess room just as the pudding arrived. Insubordination was punished by confinement on bread and water, usually in the detached or isolation hospital. Solitary confinement was often ordered as a means of controlling wild and disorderly behaviour. This punishment varied from being locked in one of the punishment rooms, with extra work during the hours set aside for recreation, to confinement in the 'Black Hole'. This was a small room, dank, dark and airless, situated in the basement immediately under the guardroom.

Serious cases of insubordination had to be dealt with by the Lieutenant Governor, as did the crime of 'drinking'. Forbidden to introduce any form of liquor into the College, cadets would break bounds to visit the local hostelries, all too often with the result that they were put 'on orders' and summarily incarcerated, whilst persistent offenders found themselves detained during the vacation. For the most serious cases the Governor reserved for himself several options: suspending the cadet's qualification for commissioning (with consequent loss of seniority); recommending to the Commander-in-Chief that the cadet should be publicly expelled, 'as not likely to profit from further residence', or, in extreme cases, 'barred from the Service for a period of two to four years'. The latter phrase meant that the ex-cadet could not then buy a commission during this period of time. Lesser awards by the Governor included rustication in term time or detention during the vacation. Of those who survived – and many probably thrived on the system – it must be said that the unending struggle between the College authorities and the gentlemen cadets must have inculcated in the latter the invaluable qualities of constant alertness and a high sense of self-preservation.

CHAPTER 5

Committees, Canteens and Cricket

CRIMEAN CRISIS

When the Crimean War broke out in 1853 there were 195 cadets at Woolwich and 178 at Sandhurst. Both colleges were on very tight budgets and Sandhurst was certainly not in a position to meet the sudden demand for junior officers to fill vacancies and replace casualties. The two technical corps were able to make up the number of young officers needed in the Crimea by direct commissioning from the universities or elsewhere, but for Sandhurst the situation was quite different. Almost without exception young men being commissioned into the Cavalry and Guards entered by the purchase system, as also did many who went to the Line Regiments, and for these to pass through the RMC was very much the exception. For instance, the number of commissions by purchase from Sandhurst in the early 1850s averaged 43 a year. Moreover the number of free commissions from Sandhurst had been cut back in recent years. In the first year of the war, however, 95 RMC cadets were commissioned, and of these commissions only 11 were by purchase. To place this in perspective, the number of young officers required to replace the casualties in the Cavalry and Infantry in 1855 was 1,378, of which the Line Regiments took 258 by purchase and 949 without purchase, the majority being by direct commissioning.

In the same two opening years of the war the Royal Military Academy was able to provide 70 and 83 young officers for the two technical corps, compared with an average of 35 for the three previous years. This exodus was balanced by large entries of 78 and 96, which by 1856 brought the numbers under instruction up to 200.

In his history of Sandhurst Brigadier Sir John Smyth comments on the situation at this date: 'The nation gets the Army it deserves – or is prepared to pay for!' It had taken the fears and tribulations of the 'Great European War' against Napoleon to bring to fruition Le Marchant's scheme for a national military college, but during the long years of peace many of his original concepts had been abandoned, or had withered for want of proper financial support and been thrown away. Sandhurst at this time of real crisis was half empty, understaffed and paralysed through lack of funds.

Between 1855 and 1857 a select committee and no less than two commissions ploughed backwards and forwards over the wastelands of Sandhurst's recent past, assisted by such experienced officers as Sir Howard Douglas, whose outspoken advice could no longer be ignored. Many of their deliberations were focused on the role of the Senior Department. The result was that the Staff College came into being as a separate establishment with its own building in a corner of the Sandhurst estate. Whereas the staff had shrunk to John Narrien and one other professor, there was now to be a Commandant, Adjutant and nine professors, and the number of students was to be increased to thirty. The new home for the Staff College was not ready until 1862 and up to this date the staff and students continued to live and work in the west wing of the RMC.

THE DRIFT TOWARDS AMALGAMATION

In 1856 Major General Sir Harry Jones took over from General Sir George Scovell as Governor. Harry Jones was a distinguished Royal Engineer officer who had been in charge of the siege operations before Sevastopol. In spite of being severely wounded he had continued to supervise the work personally, being carried about the battlefield on a litter. He certainly was a man who knew how to get things done, and within months of his taking command approval was given for a number of long-overdue improvements to be put in hand at an overall cost of £12,000. Briefly, these included the installation of gas throughout the College, improvements to the kitchens, the fitting-up of two rooms for baths and installing lavatories with hot and cold water at the ends of the two dormitory corridors. From this it seems that the authorities in London were beginning to take some notice of the College and its requirements.

One War Office letter requested urgent attention. 'When, for what reason and by whose authority the swimming master at the RMC was discontinued? . . . as the subject will be brought before the House of Commons on Friday next.' In his reply the Governor was able to indicate that in 1812 an armourer and a shoemaker had been paid out of College funds to give part-time instruction, but 'since the removal of the College from Marlow no payment has been made on this account'! He might well have added that the College funds could no longer run to such extravagances.

In reporting on the Cadet College the Select Committee seems to have avoided making any recommendations except that the orphan class should be restored under the new name of Queen's Cadetships. The task of revising the College regulations thus fell on the newly formed Council for

Military Education. The age for entry was raised to between fifteen and seventeen, and then changed to between sixteen and nineteen. The course was to be of two years' duration, culminating in a two-day written examination in London at Burlington House, in contrast to the traditional oral examination held at the College. It was also decided that 'the education of gentlemen for all Arms of the Service who do not obtain commissions by direct appointment shall be given at Sandhurst', while on the other hand cadets who failed to qualify could still take the examination for direct commissioning at a later date!

In January 1858 the first competitive examination for entry to Sandhurst was held, but the number of applicants had been lower than ever before. The number of cadets at the College had in fact reached the peacetime 'low' of twenty years before. In February an attempt was made to attract more sons of serving officers by reducing the fees and placing no limit on the number in that category. In April a letter to the Governor from the War Office contained the following paragraph: 'As the amalgamation of the Academy and the College has been decided on, General Peel considers it important that the regulations of the two establishments should be assimilated as far as possible . . .'

SEPOY INTERVENTION

Many thousands of miles away, however, the future of Sandhurst was being decided at the storming of Lucknow and the Battle of Gwalior. By June the Mutiny had been crushed, although it was another twelve months before the last band of rebellious native troops had been rounded up. As Sir John Fortescue writes in *The History of the British Army*, 'The principal result of the Mutiny was that the government of India was transferred from the East India Company to the Crown, and the 24,000 British troops in the Company's service to the Queen's Army.' Although the Company's college at Addiscombe was not finally closed for another three years, the need to increase the numbers under instruction both at Woolwich and at Sandhurst was patently obvious and a matter of urgency.

For Sandhurst, it was the start of a new era. As far as officer recruitment was concerned, the immediate effect of the absorption of the European units of the East India Company was that the Queen's Regiment and the next twenty-three Line Regiments were augmented by a second battalion. Again a nucleus of British officers would now have to be found for the 150 Indian cavalry regiments and infantry battalions, plus 86 batteries of native artillery and some 15 companies of sappers and miners, whose officers had previously been recruited by 'John Company' (the East India Company) and in many cases trained at Addiscombe.

A Policy for Expansion

Seemingly unaware of this situation, the Treasury continued to quibble over the size of the annual vote for Woolwich and Sandhurst, complaining in particular that the reduced fees and extra free places at Sandhurst ran contrary to its policy of self-sufficiency. But meanwhile the War Office had reversed its policy of eventually amalgamating the RMA and RMC and announced its intention of abolishing direct commissioning, and was at that very moment calling urgently for plans to increase the accommodation at both cadet establishments. At Woolwich the result was the building of two new wings, providing nearly a hundred cadets' single rooms, together with extra classrooms and officers' quarters. A gymnasium and a school of arms were added to the training facilities and the total cost of the new construction came to just under £58,000.

At Sandhurst the situation was complicated by the fact that the Staff College was still using much of the accommodation. The Governor reported that when the student officers moved out there would be room for 375 cadets and 93 officers, professors, other ranks and servants, and these would be the absolutely maximum numbers. At this point the War Office

The Professors at the RMA Woolwich in 1869, sketched by Gentleman Cadet
L.G. Fawkes. Royal Artillery Institution.

was planning for 500 cadets, but this figure was soon adjusted to 400, a proportion of whom would be in single rooms. The construction of extra wings built on at the back of the College started immediately, and the first to be completed was temporarily given over to the Staff College.

The new accommodation, complete with extra classrooms and stores, provided rooms for under officers but cubicles for the cadets. The latter were partitioned to within 2 foot 9 inches (84 cm) of the ceiling and were bitterly cold. Heating by hot-water pipes had been installed but the apparatus was of the most elementary description and quite unable to cope with a Herculean task. The staircases led straight down into the basement, and at the end of each corridor the large windows were kept permanently open. The result was a steady flow of cold air, and the temperature in winter could remain around freezing for days on end. It seems also that the new washrooms often flooded. John Parrant, a College servant looking after twenty-three young gentlemen, recalled that 'the cadets used to take their cans and just throw the water over themselves anyhow, and we servants, as we came back from breakfast, were often met by water pouring down the steps, and we had to collect it in cans and scoops'. The plumbing in the 'new buildings' had in fact been faulty from the start. Much to the distress and inconvenience of the unfortunate occupants of the basement, this situation continued for six or seven years before money was eventually voted to have proper waste pipes installed.

SEEDS OF MUTINY

Outwardly both Woolwich and Sandhurst were changing quite dramatically – one could say 'growing up' – in that the new accommodation would give better conditions as well as provide for more cadets. To see the buildings near completion must have given the staff the comfortable reassurance that the well-regulated daily routine would soon be re-established. It is strange that those responsible for planning this daily routine, and watching over the whole process of turning young men into officers, seemed to be oblivious of the fact that the regulations themselves were out of step with the changes that had taken place under their very eyes.

Much has been written about the 'mutinies' that occurred in the early 1860s. Both of these incidents point the moral that grown men react unfavourably to being treated as schoolboys. This of itself is a lesson in leadership. For in a military establishment the proper maintenance of discipline is a *sine qua non*. The respective Governors had in fact failed in their appreciation of the situation; but one suspects their attitude was that of *laissez-faire*.

63

At Woolwich at this particular period the cadet entry was a complete hotchpotch. Some were admitted by nomination, some by the new competitive examination, others transferred from Addiscombe and even from Sandhurst; all were of different ages and at different stages of instruction. This situation was worsened by the fact that many of those who had most recently joined were as old as nineteen, had no previous experience of military discipline, did not intend to stay at the Academy long, and were consequently intractable when they joined and naturally rebellious. The corporals on the other hand, who had all the power, were often much younger, having been promoted from the younger and earlier intakes. To the older cadets the severity of the punishments for comparatively small irregularities, and particularly for the 'crime' of smoking, seemed oppressive and only suitable for mere boys.

The trouble started at breakfast on a cold October morning in 1861 with a demonstration against the disgusting characteristics of the eggs that were being served. In class the corporals found it impossible to curb the unrest. Then battalion drill was ordered. A bitter north wind swept the parade ground and a cadet who dropped his rifle was promptly put under arrest. The germ of an 'illegal combination' was born and every minute or so a rifle or busby would fall. The time for dinner came and passed, and the numbers under arrest soared. When the call for afternoon study sounded it was ignored and the company officers were forced to order each cadet individually to go to his classroom. The Governor then announced that a court of inquiry would be held and meanwhile ordered that all the under officers and corporals be placed under arrest.

Feeling that their grievances would now be aired, most of the cadets were ready to settle down to a quiet life. A few militants, however, were not content to wait for any proper investigation and continued to indulge in a series of escapades. The most notorious of these took place after supper one night, when a party of cadets 'ran one of the fieldguns down to the front parade, loaded it with a charge smuggled up from the Arsenal under a cloak, rammed a loaf of bread down the bore, and fired it off in the direction of the Governor's house'. This and several other incidents were promptly dealt with by rusticating the ringleaders and the whole Company was punished by being confined to barracks for the remaining five weeks of term. This was an unfortunate decision as the workshops, gymnasium and racquet courts had all been demolished to make way for the new accommodation wings. The result was that many cadets, confined without any means of recreation for weeks on end, took to drinking, playing cards and breaking out at every opportunity.

At this stage HRH The Commander-in-Chief intervened. He sent the

Adjutant General down to address the whole Academy on parade and, having made his grave displeasure at the disturbances clear, was sensible enough to concede that some changes in the regulations might be considered. On his orders the ten corporals most involved were rusticated and this was the end of the affair.

Recollections of a College Servant

Almost exactly a year later a somewhat similar series of incidents occurred at Sandhurst. It is perhaps of some significance that official correspondence of this date is missing, but a reference occurs two months later, in December 1862, when the Military Secretary asked for the names of those on the list submitted for commissioning who had been concerned in the 'late refractory proceedings at the College'. John Parrant was at that time a private servant to the Lieutenant Governor and recalls:

Colonel Scott was called 'Ginger Wig' by the cadets. He was a very stern man, and so too was Sir Harry Jones, the Governor. I think it was their severe discipline which caused the 'mutiny', which I remember well. The cadets shut themselves up in the redoubt which stood on the site of the present Round Ground, and they refused to come out until they were persuaded by one of the other officers. Two or three fires broke out in the College, but they were discovered before any real damage was done. On one occasion I was carrying tea upstairs from the basement in Colonel Scott's house when the cadets started to break the windows and stones came flying round my head.

Parrant also remembers that when he was first employed at the College, four or five years previously, 'the feeding of the cadets was very bad; only a small portion of meat and bread was served out to each cadet, and he had no chance of getting any more. The coffee came up in pails, and was poured into basins for the cadets. The whole table service and meals were very rough and ready, and not at all comfortable.'

A Miserable Diet

It is interesting to find amongst the College records that by the early 1860s a new diet had been approved, much play being made of the fact that, by comparison with Woolwich, the Sandhurst cadet got 'unlimited' servings at dinner and pudding every day, instead of occasionally. Details of the Sandhurst timetable and the new diet are as follows: Rouse, 7.10, followed by inspection and prayers, with breakfast from 8 to 8.25; study and parade from 8.40 to 1.50; dinner from 2 to 2.30, followed by two hours for recreation. Study then continued until 8.30 in the evening, with supper from 6.30 to 7. At 8.30 the cadets were locked in for the night. The diet cost 1s. 8⅜d. a day. Breakfast was coffee, sugar, milk, bread and butter. Dinner provided meat, vegetables, pudding, bread and small beer. Supper was the same as breakfast, but with tea instead of coffee. Regardless of the much publicised comparison with the RMA, this was a miserable diet for young men who were in their early twenties, the upper age for entry having been raised to twenty-two for the cavalry and twenty for infantry candidates. Setting aside the restrictive regulations and almost total lack of facilities for recreation, the bad and insufficient food had become the cadets' principal grievance.

A SIEGE

The redoubt, which has long since been demolished, stood between the present boathouse and the Kurnool Mortar. Here provisions to withstand a siege had been secreted. The day came when the cadets were all ordered on extra drill. Instead of parading under arms they assembled under the corporals and marched down to the redoubt. The authorities, seeing that matters had assumed a serious aspect, endeavoured to talk the mutineers into reason. 'Ginger Wig' was met with hoots and jeers and retired discomforted. Colonel Napier (the Superintendent of Studies) then tried his hand, but with little success, though he was received in a friendly spirit and his speech was lustily cheered. Eventually, the Governor agreed to listen to their grievances if the cadets would surrender and come on parade. This they did; but next day, before any redress had been offered, all the corporals were arrested; and the cadets, furious at the breach of faith, returned to the redoubt. All terms were now refused and there they remained until the arrival of HRH The Duke of Cambridge. Although his words were probably long remembered by many, they have gone unrecorded, and perhaps were best not printed. His style, however, has been described as 'inimitable'. Order having been quickly restored, the Duke gave instructions that the corporals should be released and reinstated in their rank. So ended this affray, except of course for the post-mortems.

CONFLICTS ON COMPROMISE

At first Sir Harry Jones assumed that some relaxation of the College regulations would ease the tension. The Duke, however, was quick to remark, after the end-of-term parade the following December, that there was a deterioration in the standard of drill and turnout of the cadets. Both the Governor and Colonel Scott now felt that their former rigid attitude on disciplinary matters was officially supported. Orders were given that the loss of 'conduct marks' could lead to delay in commissioning or even removal from the College. The Governor himself strongly held to the

Prince Albert inspecting the Royal Horse Artillery on Woolwich Common in front of the Royal Military Academy. RMA Sandhurst Collection.

Cadet Races at the RMA Woolwich. From a painting by G.B. Campion, 1850. RMA Sandhurst Collection.

The Duke of Cambridge presenting prizes at the RMA Woolwich in 1860. From a drawing by G.B. Campion. RMA Sandhurst Collection.

The Great Fire at the Academy in 1873. From a contemporary painting. RMA Sandhurst Collection.

view that cadets should be kept busy and given little or no opportunity of getting into trouble when off parade; nor was he prepared to make room in the daily programme for innovations.

As part of the building programme the gymnasium (now the Central Library) had just been completed. It was, however, hardly being used at all and such instruction as did take place was being ordered during the cadets' afternoon recreational break between classes. Again the Duke had to intervene and order a compromise solution. Two periods of gymnastics each week during the first six months of the course could be held in the afternoons, but a third period must take place during programme hours in place of an hour's drill; then during the second six months, instruction in fencing and singlestick would replace the former compulsory periods. It was subsequently discovered that the College authorities translated these instructions by allocating a mere twenty minutes between the fourth study period and tea for gymnastics and fencing, and this included the time taken by the cadets to march to and from the gymnasium.

If anything, the restrictions on the cadets' free time were increasing, as for instance when the Governor insisted, after a somewhat heated correspondence with the War Office, that lights out should be at 9 p.m. His argument supporting this proposal was that the expense of gas lighting would be saved. It is far more likely that Colonel Scott wanted to make it more difficult for cadets to break out for visits to the local hostelries.

A New Commandant

Shortly after these happenings Colonel Scott was promoted and sent to the Channel Islands as one of the Governors. The title of Lieutenant Governor was now dropped and his successor as Commandant was Colonel Halliwell. While discipline was probably just as strict, there was now a change of attitude towards amenities and recreational facilities for the cadets. The upper age for entry was also fixed at nineteen for all cadets, and an extra six months, on top of the one year's course, could be allowed to enable cadets to qualify for a non-purchase commission. As for amenities, the first proposal was to build a skittle alley next to the gymnasium, where smoking would also be allowed. Instead three rooms and a store in the basement of the College were set aside to provide billiard and smoking rooms and a 'canteen' for the sale of beer and light refreshments. The billiard tables were bought from Government funds, but any subsequent repair of the tables had to be paid for by the cadets. It seems that the Secretary of State also authorised the purchase of six spittoons at a cost of $1s. 1\frac{1}{2}d.$ each, and it is to be hoped that he had no sleepless nights over this wild expenditure of public funds.

Certainly money was saved in another direction as a request that the wooden forms used in the dining halls should be replaced by chairs was promptly turned down. On the other hand there was at long last a move to encourage organised sport. In 1865 a proper cricket ground was constructed in front of the gymnasium. This became known as the Round Ground, and in modern times is often used by the Sandhurst Wanderers. The cost turned out to be £128. 18s. 1d., somewhat in excess of the estimated £100. The itemised account mentions that 10,650 turfs were carted by contract from Windsor Park; 60 tons of chalk were brought from Guildford; and 20 tons of manure had to be collected from Aldershot.

VARIOUS EVILS AND THEIR REMEDY

Progress in this and other sports will shortly be described, but meanwhile the discipline at the cadet colleges was still under discussion at high levels. General Sir John Burgoyne, shortly to be promoted to Field Marshal, was Constable of the Tower. He had served under Moore at Corunna and throughout the Peninsular War and was now asked for his advice. His memorandum 'Outbreaks at the Royal Military Academies' presumably reflected the views of many of his generation. He saw the main cause of the trouble as stemming from the harshness and overbearing attitude of the officers, while poor messing and 'ill-timed regulations affecting the hours appropriated to recreation' were contributory factors. Turning to the recent innovation of refreshment rooms, he had nothing good to say. Smoking he regarded as an 'unnecessary habit, one that is expensive, and an indulgence that can never benefit, but may be deleterious to health, therefore I would suggest that though allowed it should not be encouraged'. If the cadets were properly fed, a 'canteen' was unnecessary and 'ale, porter and stimulating drinks [tea and coffee] are absolutely injurious'.

It is of interest that these strictures were promptly endorsed by the Council for Military Education as well as by a former Superintendent of Studies at Sandhurst, who wrote: 'Anything like a compromise with idle or dissipated habits, such as those of beer-drinking and smoking at irregular hours, must be inconsistent with sound morality. I say the same of billiards.'

Colonel Halliwell, however, was not to be deterred in pressing for recognition of the modest reforms so recently introduced. It was hardly necessary, he felt, to point out that young men were always hungry, and in any case for the last fifty years the 'Tuck Barrow', which arrived from the village and appeared in front of the College during recreation hours, had always been surrounded by cadets even in wet weather. How much better to have a room in the College to serve the same purpose, where cadets

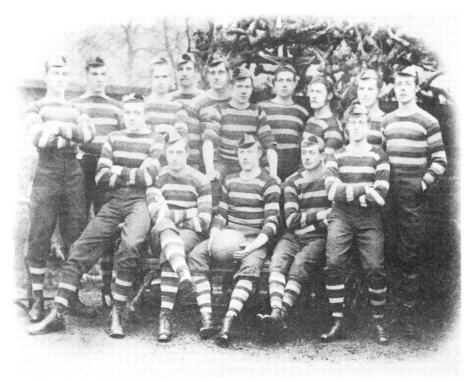

RMA Rugby XV in 1875.

could also entertain their friends in a modest and economical manner. He had in mind the serving of cold fowls, hares, meat pies, sweets and ices. As for the sale of beer, this was practically always drunk with lemonade, and was it not proof enough of the success of the innovation that the local publicans were all now complaining of the loss of custom?

At this point the Duke stepped in and orders were received that the recreation rooms were to be enlarged.

ON RECREATION

General Burgoyne's report concluded with a strong plea for an increase in other means of recreation, for which competitive prizes might be given. He gave priority to 'all outdoor manly exercise, cricket, football, racquets, boating, swimming, quoits, rifle practice, gymnastics, etc., etc. [For indoors:] billiards, chess, covered court racquets, artificiers' workshops, modelling, gymnastics in covered halls, reading rooms for light literature, etc., etc.' There is little doubt that Colonel Halliwell was already quietly working on many of these ideas. The cricket ground was under construction; a shipwright had come from Woolwich to repair the boats (many of which were found to be beyond redemption); the billiards and recreation rooms were a going concern, and one of the company commanders was trying to set up a reading room for the cadets. Apropos of the reading room, it seems that the Governor was not being very helpful as he had turned down a request for a small sum to be spent on having the room decorated with wallpaper. The proposals for workshops and modelling, already popular at Woolwich, were also turned down as inappropriate for the Sandhurst cadets.

Earlier in the summer of the same year the first of the annual cricket matches against the RMA had taken place. This was played at Lords and the Academy won by an innings and 174 runs, a result that drew from the Duke the brief comment that he hoped the College would produce a stronger team next time. It is strange that General Burgoyne made no mention of athletics. Traditionally the 'Annual Games' at Sandhurst used to be held on the Round Ground and became very much of a social event spread over two days, and before the cricket ground was constructed it is doubtful if there were facilities for such an event. At Woolwich, however, athletic sports were well established.

EARDLEY-WILMOT AND THE BUGLE

Any review of sport at the cadet colleges must pay tribute to Captain F.W. Eardley-Wilmot, who commanded the Cadet Company at the Academy from 1847 to 1854. It was he who had been responsible for a number of improvements in the life of the cadets, such as the introduction of workshops for their use, but he is remembered more particularly for his interest in and encouragement of their games. In 1849, under his direction, the RMA Sports was inaugurated – the first athletics meeting ever to be held in England. The following year Eardley-Wilmot presented a silver bugle as a trophy to be competed for annually. At first the name of the cadet winning the greatest number of events was inscribed on the bugle itself; later silver coins were attached to links on a chain for the same purpose. With the outbreak of the Crimean War the event lapsed, but it was revived with the arrival of the Addiscombe batch in 1862.

In 1868 inter-collegiate athletic sports were instituted between the RMA and the RMC and a shield was presented by the two Governors. The first meeting was held at Beaufort House, Fulham, and was won by the Academy by nine events to three. After only two more years this annual event lapsed for nearly a decade owing to the changed conditions at Sandhurst. From then until the turn of the century the records show that, in spite of the RMC having more cadets and their being somewhat older, honours were equally divided between the two establishments.

Rugby football was started at the Shop in the early 1860s. Colours were awarded in 1867, in which year a challenge was issued to Sandhurst. This was turned down on the pretext that the date did not fit into the programme, but the truth probably was that the RMC could not raise a team. The first recorded fixtures for a Sandhurst representative Rugby team were against the Indian College of Engineering, Coopers Hill, and the Royal Naval College, Greenwich, and took place in 1874. Two years later, the inter-collegiate series was started, with the Academy winning the first

Captain Eardley-Wilmot presenting the 'Bugle' at the annual athletics meeting at the Shop. From a drawing by G.B. Campion.

fixture. Over the years, however, the slightly older Sandhurst cadets – and there were more to choose from – had an advantage. Of the first twenty-four matches Sandhurst won fourteen, with Woolwich winning five and four games being drawn.

In those days Association football was less popular than it is now, certainly as far as the Army was concerned. The first outside fixture arranged by an RMC team was against Eton in 1876. Colours were awarded two years later. 'Red and blue quartered shirt and cap, white knickerbockers, one red and one blue stocking. A little later in the same year, red and white was substituted for red and blue, the stockings to be striped.' The fixture list for 1879–80 includes Charterhouse, Eton, Winchester and Bradfield College, the Old Harrovians and the Old Carthusians, as well as the Royal Engineers and Reading. Five matches were won, two lost and four drawn.

At Woolwich there was a good deal of resistance to the introduction of the game. The Recreation Committee of 1881 indeed decided that 'there would be no objection to the Association team, provided the following suggestions were carried out: i. The Association team not to be entitled to wear the Academy colours. ii. Not to play Sandhurst. iii. Not to be called the RMA Association Team, but by the name of the gentleman who manages, or gets it up, such as "Mr Parry's team". iv. The Rugby team always to have choice of days and grounds', and so on, with further restrictions on fixtures and dates. It was seven years before the Governor would agree to a fixture being arranged with the RMC, which the Shop won by a goal to nil, and up to 1900 they retained this one-game lead over the College.

A game that was always popular with the cadets was racquets. The first of the matches between the RMA and the RMC was played in 1879, when honours were divided between the singles and doubles. Although Woolwich produced some outstanding players in both events, such as A. Cooper-Key, S.H. Shephard and W.L. Foster, Sandhurst gradually drew ahead in the overall number of wins.

In the *Annals of Sandhurst* mention is made of hockey having been played for a number of years until it was superseded by football, to be resuscitated only in the late 1890s. A polo club was in existence during the late seventies and eighties and was supported by both officers and cadets, although the number involved was never more than twenty. The football ground was used to start with, and then the riding field. Later a field was rented near Wellington College, but with increased afternoon studies this ground was really too far distant. The Commander-in-Chief had in fact already decided that the game encouraged extravagance, and the club was closed down in 1894.

In this latter part of the century, as will soon be noted, several other sports and activities were introduced at both colleges. Meanwhile official attitudes towards the physical fitness of the newly joined cadet produced a somewhat bizarre situation. In 1878 the Civil Service Commission, which was responsible for the entrance examinations to both colleges, drew up proposals to allocate marks for proficiency in any three of the following: riding, walking, running, leaping, swimming and putting the shot. Running a mile in $5\frac{1}{2}$ minutes, for instance, would earn 100 marks, but doing it in 5 minutes would earn 400 marks. The scheme was debated in the House of Lords, and might well have been approved but for the intervention of the Press, who made great play of the difficulties and amusing scenes that would result in marking some two hundred candidates. Sir John Adye, the Governor of the RMA, had in fact opposed the scheme 'as likely to induce lads to go into training and neglect their studies'.

RMC Polo Club in 1885.

CHAPTER 6

Victorian Reformers

SANDHURST UNDER ATTACK

Over the years rivalry in sport between the Shop and Sandhurst grew and
became very much a feature of life at both colleges, but had a vote in the
House of Commons gone the other way in 1866 all this might have been
different. Harking back to the 'mutinies', Lord Eustace Cecil launched an
attack on practically every aspect of life and work at the colleges and particularly at Sandhurst. In his speech he claimed both were over-staffed. The
entrance examination at Woolwich was too difficult and that at Sandhurst
too selective. Both Addiscombe and West Point had been able to supply
officers for every branch of the Service, so surely one college would 'meet
the requirements for our small army, more especially as the majority
of officers were admitted by means of direct commission'. Furthermore,
there would then be a considerable saving of public money. Woolwich and
Sandhurst 'were neither barracks, schools, nor colleges, but institutions
combining the faults of all three', and they should be subjected to a full
inquiry by a royal commission.

   Those supporting the motion seem to have been concerned mainly with
questions of discipline and the need, as they saw it, for amalgamation. Mr
Acland, however, had visited Sandhurst and took the view that a good
liberal education was the best preparation for entering the Army. Sir James
Fergusson pointed out that the competitive examination for Woolwich
had 'attracted to the annual competition some of the best taught young
men in all the great schools of England'. In France, Prussia and nearly
every other country in Europe 'persons desiring to enter the Army were
obliged to submit themselves to the special education provided for them at
military academies, and he thought the House would be wrong to discourage a course of instruction which had so far been attended with the
best possible results'. The Marquess of Hartington pointed out that, only
a few years before, a commission of inquiry had gone into the whole
question of military education. The proposal to amalgamate the two
establishments had at that time been rejected by the House and 'the

inquiries show that the present system has worked very well upon the whole'.

General Peel then spoke. He considered all officers should attend a military college, not just to learn their drill, which was a secondary consideration, but so that the Army might 'learn the character of the man before he gets his commission, as afterwards it is a very difficult matter to get rid of him without going before a court martial'. While the high standard of the Sandhurst entrance examination was necessary because of the competition to gain a commission without purchase, not sufficient free commissions were being offered. Hence the number of applicants was falling off.

When put to the vote, the motion for the appointment of a royal commission was defeated by 152 votes to 132. Only a few years later, however, there were many far-reaching reforms of the Army as a whole, which in the end stabilised the role and status of the cadet colleges.

THE CARDWELL REFORMS

Between 1868 and 1874 Lord Cardwell was Secretary for War in Gladstone's first administration. One of the reforms for which Cardwell is often remembered is the abolition of the purchase of commissions in the Army, but this was only one of a whole series of measures linked to a common aim. Briefly, the reforms involved merging Horse Guards (the office of the Commander-in-Chief) and the War Office; the introduction of short service to build up a reserve; the transfer of control of the Militia, Yeomanry and Volunteers to the Crown, combined with the organisation of the United Kingdom into military districts commanding all regular and auxiliary forces; the abolition of purchase; and other measures such as the linking of infantry regiments to improve the conditions of overseas service.

On the question of purchase the reality of the situation was that once the regular and auxiliary forces had been brought together 'into one harmonious and compact body', it had to be made possible for the regular officers to serve with the reserve forces, in which the purchase system had never existed and would never be accepted. The purchase system therefore had to go. The practice of recruiting officers by purchase did not exist in the Royal Navy, Royal Marines, Royal Artillery or Royal Engineers. In the remainder of the Army, however, and without including the Guards or colonial units, the 'purchase corps' totalled 169, i.e. regiments of cavalry, battalions of infantry and the Military Train.

When the proposal to abolish purchase became known there was considerable resistance from the large number of officers who, with no pension to look forward to, had 'invested' considerable sums in what was in reality a saleable commodity, especially at the time of their retirement. Even after it was made clear that compensation would be paid, the question of over-regulation payments bedevilled the passage of the bill, but eventually, in October 1871, a royal warrant was issued setting out the new regulations for first appointments and regimental promotion. The royal warrant was framed on the principle of seniority tempered by selection – the aim was that competence should be the criterion for all appointments and pro-motions. The ranks of cornet and ensign for the Cavalry and Infantry were done away with. All first appointments would now be as sub-lieutenants for a probationary period of three years. At the end of this period, if the young officer was not qualified for promotion, he would have to leave the service. Commissions would be free, carry the right to a pension and be obtained by competition.

Owing to the resistance to the introduction of these proposals, or rather to the abolition of the former system of purchase, there were long delays in passing the necessary legislation by the Regulation of the Forces Act, and the War Office plans for the transitionary period went seriously awry.

SUB-LIEUTENANTS TAKE OVER

The decision to close down Sandhurst as a cadet college had already been implemented. By the beginning of 1870 only a single batch of cadets remained and no more were joining. Only a handful of the staff remained. Meanwhile direct commissions were being offered through the competitive examination and the number of successful candidates was building up. Until the royal warrant was signed, however, none of these were able to take up their commissions and the expediency of appointing them as sub-lieutenants unattached had to be adopted. In February 1871 a course was arranged for the top hundred of the sub-lieutenants at Sandhurst while the remainder were sent to live with regiments and attend garrison schools. The Sandhurst batch were known as gentlemen students and for all intents and purposes were volunteers for the course. When the last of the cadets left, however, further batches of sub-lieutenants were ordered to join the RMC, being crammed in until the College was bursting at the seams. As they had to be treated as officers, as far as possible each had to be given a room, but by the beginning of 1875 there were 225 in residence, plus 24 university students and 20 Queen's Cadets. Even with the use of the Terrace for officers' quarters, many of the students sleeping in the College were put three to a room in the old large rooms that had formerly taken four cadets.

Each course lasted a year: eight months' work spread over three terms.

Group of sub-lieutenants at the RMC in 1873.

The syllabus that eventually emerged was directly related to the examination that all must pass to earn their commissions as lieutenants. There were six sections: Queen's Regulations, regimental interior economy, accounts and correspondence; military law; elements of tactics; field fortifications and elements of permanent fortifications; military topography and reconnaissance; and riding. The students were drilled by their divisional officers and later by drill sergeants loaned from Aldershot. The College regulations were eventually rewritten, and as an incentive to students to study and pass out high on the list for promotion to lieutenant an antedate system was introduced – two years for those in the top of three grades, one year for those in the middle grade and none for those in the bottom grade.

The fact that the course was undoubtedly conducted more efficiently than within the garrisons meant little to the majority of the gentlemen students. They still had to answer rollcall at 10 p.m. and the gas lights were turned off an hour later, although the students were then allowed to have 'private' lights in their rooms. The sub-lieutenants all wore a simple and unadorned blue patrol uniform supplemented only by a scarlet shell jacket and mess vest, and an infantry-pattern greatcoat. For a brief period 'regimentals', the more colourful uniforms approved for the various regiments, were allowed, but this concession was quickly rescinded. The Government *per capita* grant to cover messing and the expense of running the College laundry was 3s. 6d. a day. When the first batch of student officers arrived there was still a restriction on the allowance for pocket money. This was probably raised, but for the Queen's Cadets it was 2s. 6d. a week as previously.

There is little doubt that this was a very testing time for the Governor and his attenuated staff. Harry Jones had died 'in the saddle' in the summer of 1866, and was buried in the College cemetery with considerable ceremony. In the College Chapel a tablet erected in his memory recorded the twelve engagements in which had taken part, from Walcheren in 1809 to Sevastopol forty-six years later. His successor, General Sir G.H. Wetherall, died within two years, at the age of eighty, after a long illness. Lieutenant General Sir D.A. Cameron, KCB, of the 42nd Foot was then appointed, with the unenviable task of implementing the changes just described.

A glance through correspondence emanating from the Governor's office during the sub-lieutenant era shows some of the problems. There were too few instructors; the standard of riding of many of the young officers joining the Cavalry was far too low; the Governor was gravely concerned over the poor standard of elementary arithmetic and geometry; the report on the gymnastics course was fairly satisfactory but the attendance at voluntary classes was less than 6 per cent and for fencing only 1.3 per cent and so on month by month. Nor was the War Office always helpful, as evidenced when the Adjutant General's office wrote: 'Please inform me what is the colour of the tuft in Adjutant's chaco.' The Governor's reply, written no doubt more in pain than anger, was: 'There is no Adjutant at the College, the appointment having been abolished.' More serious was the fact that the course itself was not popular; the institutional life, even under the relaxed conditions, was anathema to young men who saw themselves as trapped in an artificial environment where as officers, even in embryo, they had nothing to command. Discipline consequently suffered.

FRIVOLOUS COMPLAINTS

A further complication arose from the fact that an increasingly high proportion of the sub-lieutenants sent to Sandhurst came from the Household Troops and the Cavalry and that the final examinations of these young officers were taking place, not at Sandhurst, but at their regimental headquarters or depots. The anomaly of this situation was brought out into the open when some of the officers complained that they had not been taught at the RMC the subjects on which they were subsequently examined. On investigation this claim proved to be quite without foundation. The Governor was incensed and considered 'that the complaint in question was a discreditable attempt on the part of these officers to excuse their ignorance of subjects in which, but for their persistent idleness, they had every opportunity of being fully instructed'. The Governor continued by reminding the War Office that eight out of the ten officers concerned had been amongst those who, on the occasion of the Commander-in-Chief's recent visit, had 'preferred frivolous complaints against the division officers', and that earlier in the year there had been a particularly serious outbreak of ill discipline and all four division officers on the staff had tendered their resignations. The Field Marshal, however, had refused to allow the resignations to go through and now gave instructions that if the young officers in question did not come to heel they were to be sent back to their regiments with a view to their being dismissed the Service. Furthermore, those who had failed the recent preliminary examination 'owing to negligence and inattention at study and whose conduct has been so unfavourably prominent' should be told that 'if they fail again, removal from the Army will be the inevitable result'.

GENTLEMEN CADETS RETURN TO SANDHURST

In 1875 Sir Duncan Cameron was in the last year of his appointment as Governor. It was a year of modest but solid progress. Although he still had no adjutant, nine more instructors had been posted to his staff. A new riding course had been approved. His suggestion that detachments from Aldershot should be sent over to demonstrate tactical lessons had also been approved. An issue of 250 Martini Henry rifles had arrived to replace the obsolescent Snider rifles. Another accommodation wing was being built, and money had been voted for a new chapel and the site chosen.

We now come to a turning point in the history of Sandhurst. While the RMA had been spared the uprooting of an established system, the RMC had suffered from years of uncertainty and disorder. A simple evolutionary step was now to restore at least a climate of stability and provide objectives at once clearly defined and critical to the commissioning of all regular officers, other than those entering the technical branches of the Army.

The War Office, having assumed responsibility for the affairs of the College under a royal warrant of 1876, straight away dispensed with the Board of Commissioners. The Sandhurst Committee was now the sole advisory body and their fourth report came out in the same year. A former member of the Committee, Lieutenant General W.C.E. Napier, had meanwhile taken over as Governor at Sandhurst.

The Committee expressed the view that a system where officers received pay and counted service towards retirement while under instruction at Sandhurst was unsound in principle and entailed unnecessary expenditure of public money. They therefore strongly recommended that all candidates for commissions, except Militia officers and promoted NCOs, should enter the College as cadets. As the cadets would be of an average age of around twenty, the general arrangements and discipline should approximate to those of the universities (rather than a school), while the military element should be duly preserved. There were to be ten divisions of twenty-five gentlemen cadets, and the details of the organisation and administration were to be based on those of the RMA. The cadets would be paid 3s. a day. Providing there was a grant of £375 a year to pay the kitchen staff, this would cover messing (including a late dinner), laundry and pocket money.

By October proposals were approved, and in February 1877 Her Majesty Queen Victoria signed a royal warrant for the future establishment of the RMC. The annual cost was estimated at £37,000, of which the Treasury expected to recoup £24,000 from the fees paid by parents and guardians, but there were to be no charges for Queen's Cadets.

THE STAFF AT SANDHURST c. 1880

It is of interest to show in detail the senior staff for Sandhurst a century ago and the cost to the taxpayer.

Superintendence		Instruction	
Governor	£1,500	1 Professor of Fortification	£500
Commandant and Secretary	£750	7 Instructors in Fortification	£2,450
Chaplain	£366	1 Professor of Surveying	£486
Officiating RC Chaplain		8 Instructors in Surveying	£2,800
(Honorarium)	£20	1 Professor of Tactics	£450
Adjutant and Quartermaster	£368	7 Instructors in Tactics	£2,450
Surgeon	£274		
Assistant Surgeon	£128		
Riding Master	£274		
7 Divisional Officers'			
Allowances	£1,000		

A strength return of 1881 prepared for the Board of Visitors gives the following details:

Staff Officers, Professors, Instructors	35
Engineer Department	14
Cadets	295
Sergeants, etc.	27
Musicians	17
Cavalry Detachment	53
Detachment of Royal Engineers	42
Civil Department	104
School*	3
(Attached as Drill Instructors	11)

Total 590 persons and 50 horses

Wanting to complete establishment: Cadets, 4; Musicians, 2

*A school for the families of NCOs, men and civilian employees had been established in the basement about forty years before.

From a separate return it seems that the entry 'Sergeants, etc.' excluded any NCOs of the Royal Engineer or Cavalry detachments, but covered the following appointments: sergeant major, quartermaster sergeant, four divisional staff sergeants, armourer sergeant, bandmaster and band sergeant, three military staff clerks, three instructors of gymnasia, sergeant compounder Army Hospital Corps, and a sergeant instructor RA. As to the wages of the civilian employees, who were described as 'civil servants, etc.', these varied from £200 a year for the chief clerk to £60 each for the housekeeper and the head cook and £40 a year for the organist. Mess waiters, cleaners and storemen were on 18s. 0d. a week, and at the bottom of the scale were the scullions and the Commandant's orderly at 10s. 6d. a week. The five gatekeepers, who presumably did long hours but lived on the job in the lodges, were paid 16s. a week. Their uniform was supplied by the College: a blue frockcoat and Oxford (i.e. grey) trousers, hence the nickname of 'Blue Bottle'.

BOOKS AND BULLETS

Another charge on the College funds was the Library. The Librarian, an appointment usually held by the Chaplain, received an allowance of £30 a year. A dozen periodicals were purchased regularly in the late 1870s. All but two, the *Quarterly Review* and the *Edinburgh Review*, were of a Service or professional nature and half of these were in either French or German.

The Library was financed by 'members' subscribing 1s. a month to borrow one book at a time for fourteen days. Opening hours for cadets were in the evening for one hour after mess, and fines for overdue books were charged at 6d. a day. Officers were allowed to borrow up to three books but had to pay bigger membership fees. The rule forbidding 'loud talking and sky-larking' presumably referred to cadets only!

As in the past, a shortage of funds, both public and private, reflected the Treasury's contention that the RMC ought to be self-sufficient. When the Governor asked the War Office to replace worn-out prayer books he received an invoice for 300 bibles on repayment, and was forced to reply: 'The requisition was for prayer books, not bibles, but as I have no means of paying for either I beg that they may not be sent.' A request for 17,000 rounds of ball ammunition for the use of the newly formed Cadets' Rifle Club resulted in an issue of 6,000 rounds. The club proved so popular that 20,000 rounds a year were needed and the cadets had to pay for the balance. It was only after several years of considerable agitation that the free allowance of rifle ammunition was increased and an issue of revolver ammunition added. When musketry was eventually introduced into the course all allowances of free ammunition for the club were quickly discontinued.

THE BIFURCATION SYSTEM AT THE RMA

In the last decades of the nineteenth century War Office control brought the two cadet establishments closer and closer together in a number of ways. The inherent difference in the educational requirements of the technical arms *vis-à-vis* the cavalry and the infantry remained. This continued to be reflected in the length of the courses. For instance, in the early 1890s, when a new system (known as bifurcation, as there were in effect different courses for the artillery and engineer cadets) was adopted at the RMA, the course, although shortened by a term, was still a two-year one. At the RMC, although the course had been lengthened, the cadets passed out in eighteen months.

Under the new bifurcation system at the Shop the decision as to whether a cadet might be commissioned as a sapper or a gunner was made on the results of the first year's examinations. During the second year the sapper cadets specialised in fortification and continued with mathematics and landscape drawing but had little artillery instruction. The gunner cadets on the other hand concentrated on artillery instruction, spent less time on fortification and did no further mathematics, while landscape drawing became a voluntary subject. Tactics and military topography, together with chemistry, were common to both courses in the second year. Mounted

THE EXPERIENCES

OF A WOOLWICH CADET

ON HIS FIRST MOUNTED RECONNAISSANCE

BY AN EYEWITNESS

1895 — 1897

Interrupted !
Q. How will this affect his scale ?

Homeward bound

*'Mounted Reconnaissance.' From a series of sketches on the
lighter side of life at the Shop, attributed to Gentleman Cadet
L.G. Fawkes. Royal Artillery Institution.*

reconnaissance was introduced in the early 1890s and quickly became the
most popular part of the whole course.

Bifurcation started in 1889 and was abandoned seven years later. The
reason for giving up the scheme was that the incentive to work for a commission in one or the other of the two corps had been removed halfway
through the course. Furthermore young officers joining the Garrison
Artillery in particular, a branch that had become increasingly scientific,
were found to be insufficiently trained for their duties.

Leaving aside for a moment the changes which were taking place in the pattern of education and training at both cadet establishments, let us glance at a few other aspects of life in late Victorian times, under the 'enlightened' cadet system, a system that some senior officers were finding it difficult to accept.

As a result of the 'Sub-Lieutenant Era' the cadets at Sandhurst had inherited a modest improvement in the furnishing of their rooms, such as an issue of carpets and rugs, while there were easychairs and card tables in the anterooms. When the Director of Artillery learned of this he put in a demand that such items should be withdrawn immediately, so as to match up, or rather down, with conditions at the RMA. Considerable correspondence of an increasingly acrimonious nature ensued. Finally the Secretary of State intervened, supporting General Napier's contention that he had been ordered to administer Sandhurst as a college for young men and not as a seminary for boys.

Ten years later it was the turn of the Academy to come under attack. At this time the President of the Board of Visitors was General Lord Airey. His report recorded the views of a member, Lieutenant General Sir J.W. Fitzmayer, who 'deprecated the luxury in which the cadets were indulged, as likely to unfit them for a military career'. The following year similar views were expressed in the Board's annual report, and this time Lord Airey added his name, taking exception to 'the absence of restraint', exemplified by such indulgences as 'balls and concerts, billiards, and smoking rooms', as well as 'the luxuries that appeared in the barrack rooms and the liberal and varied diet'. The Commander-in-Chief decided to go and see for himself. Finding all well and discipline much improved, he left the Governor to answer the criticisms and arranged for a copy of the report to be placed before Parliament. Two vacancies on the Board of Visitors occurred shortly afterwards.

One of the recommendations by the Board of Visitors that was followed up was for the enlargement of the cricket ground at Woolwich. This was carried out by filling in the ha-ha (the walled trench that had been the original boundary in front of the main buildings) and digging up the central road. Proposals that involved bricks and mortar were, however, more often shelved or set back year after year, on the pretext that the money was not available. Such was the fate of the plea that covered ways should be built from the cadets' houses at the front of the building to the bathrooms in the yard behind, and that a supply of hot water should be connected. The question of providing more single rooms was an even more urgent need, and one constantly reported as being of highest priority.

THE GREAT FIRE AT WOOLWICH

The great fire of 1873 proved a disaster in more ways than one. Not only was the central block, with the libraries and classrooms, completely burnt out, but the large sum of money that had to be spent on rebuilding might eventually have been voted to provide the extra cadet accommodation.

A civilian crossing the Common at 3 a.m. on the 1st of February had seen a light in the windows of the tower, but the alarm was not raised within the Academy by the policeman on duty until over an hour later, by which time flames were bursting through the roof. At dawn there were thirteen engines at work in the intense cold, and with no shortage of water the danger to other buildings had passed. Daylight disclosed the whole of the central block as a charred and smoking ruin rising from a sea of ice. At noon, and again the following midnight, the flames broke out afresh but they were quickly beaten down. Although some books and documents were saved, the military, history and reference libraries were entirely destroyed, together with large quantities of valuable manuscripts, official records, models and classroom equipment, at an estimated loss of over £50,000.

The origin of the fire is believed to have been a 'foul flue', and an iron ball was later found lodged in one of the flues of the heating apparatus. Up to this date the doors of the cadets' houses had been padlocked on the outside overnight, and had the fire spread more quickly many of the cadets in the adjacent houses could well have been trapped. It was now wisely decided that locks should be fitted and that the corporals should have charge of the keys. It was, however, another twenty years before the iron gratings to the windows of the cadets' houses were removed for the same reason.

A SHORTAGE OF FUNDS FOR BUILDING

In 1892 an additional block was added to the east wing, providing twenty more bedrooms, but other improvements, such as the additions of a riding school, a swimming bath and a chapel, although recommended year after year by the Board of Visitors, had been set aside for lack of funds. An indoor swimming bath was eventually built with money saved from Academy funds. The opening in 1889 was to have included a display by the celebrated Beckwith family, but had to be cancelled when it was found that the bath was leaking badly. Repairs were put in hand, and for a few months the cadets were able to enjoy their new amenity to the full. Then even more serious leaks developed, and with the money all spent, the bath had to be closed for nearly five years. The riding school was never built, and indoor classes had to take place at the regimental depot some distance away.

THE SHOP CHAPEL

The building of a chapel for the Shop was only started in 1902, over fifty years after the then Governor, Sir Lintorn Simmons, had made the initial recommendations. Twice the money had been voted, a site chosen and plans prepared. It was only after Lord Roberts had become Commander-in-Chief and himself taken up the matter with the Secretary of State that the project was brought to fruition. The Field Marshal himself laid the foundation stone, which after so many years of delays carried an apt inscription: *Nisi Dominus Frustra* – 'In vain without the Lord'.

When Sir Lintorn Simmons made the original proposal he had requested seating for 650, to cater for 'all connected with the Academy and their families'. Twenty years later the Inspector of Fortification was asked to draw up plans. He considered a seating capacity of 300 quite sufficient, although in the meantime the number of cadets had increased, but then no doubt he may have been rather more concerned over the quantity of bricks that would be needed. The Chapel, St Michael and All Angels, seats 350 and was designed by Major Hemming, RE. The altar cross, furnishings and vestments were presented by former cadets and others closely connected with the Shop.

Laying the foundation stone of the RMA Chapel in 1902.

CHAPTER 7

Swords and Medals

SPORT AND 'SWOT'

By the end of the nineteenth century the sports facilities at the RMA had been much improved. A second football pitch had been laid out behind the gymnasium and a cricket pavilion built on the recreation ground with money subscribed by the Royal Artillery and the Royal Engineers. Also a revolver range had been built on the edge of the artillery exercise ground. This proved very popular. An annual gymnastics competition against the RMC, for a shield presented by the National Physical Association, was already taking place, and in 1892 a revolver match for a challenge shield was added to the series of inter-collegiate annual events. Of the first nine matches, Woolwich won five and Sandhurst four. A prize for the best revolver shot was awarded at both colleges, and at Sandhurst there was an inter-company competition in both revolver and rifle shooting.

While recreational and training facilities were improving at both establishments, there was still a good deal of overcrowding for the Shop cadets through a shortage of single rooms. The newly joined junior cadets, or 'snookers', were worst off in every respect. They slept three to a room with distempered walls, no carpets and great bare windows. Opposite a massive iron fireplace was a huge wooden wardrobe. The only furniture was three turn-up beds, a barrack table and three hard Windsor chairs.

From reveille at 6.15 a.m. the daily programme stretched away like a fast-moving staircase, to be abruptly halted by lights out at 10.30 p.m. Before the trumpet sounded for the breakfast parade at 7.15 a.m. snatched moments of sleep would probably have left only ten minutes for the dash along the passage, no longer open to the elements, into a bath of running water (and only some of the houses had hot water), and to shave and dress. Within the hour the cadet would be at his desk for the first study, which included mathematics for both the junior classes, or he would be parading for outdoor instruction, such as military topography or field fortification. Noon brought an hour's squad or gun drill, riding or gymnastics. Lunch parade at 1.15 p.m. involved a rigorous inspection by the corporals, where a single speck of dust could bring the award of an extra drill. Then by 2.15 p.m. the cadets were out of doors again for an hour's drill, riding or artillery exercises. There followed a two-hour break in the middle of the afternoon. This might be spent on 'voluntary study' but the more fortunate were free to play games or use the excellent workshop facilities. Before the dinner parade at 7.30 p.m. there were a further two hours of study: French or German and drawing for the third and fourth classes; chemistry and physics, or tactics, military administration and law for the two senior classes.

After dinner, and until answering his name at the door of his room at 'rounds' at 10 p.m., the cadet could spend his time at voluntary classes in the workshops, or twice a week, when part of the Artillery Band played in the School of Arms, he could practise his dancing, often with rare and energetic variations quite inappropriate to any formal occasion. The billiard tables were invariably fully booked, and there were also the 'swankers' who retired to their rooms to study mathematics (known as 'swot'), chemistry (inevitably called 'stinks'), or 'GD', which stood for geometrical drawing, the subjects which provided pitfalls for many. Those fortunate cadets who had their own rooms were able to treat themselves,

Group of Academy servants, c. 1890. The livery was blue with red facings and brass buttons.

and as many friends as could be crammed in, to a 'tea squad' at which large quantities of such delicacies as the canteen could provide would be consumed.

Eventually the last days of term would come, the examinations would be over and the gymnasium would be transformed 'into a veritable palace of delight' for the final ball. Then came Public Day, with the Commander-in-Chief taking the parade, followed by demonstrations, by each class in turn, of riding, gun drill or exercises in the School of Arms.

ACCELERATION

The decision to reduce the course at Woolwich to two years had been the direct result of the demands for officers for the campaigns in Egypt and the Sudan between 1882 and 1885. Similarly at Sandhurst exceptional measures had to be adopted, 'accelerating' whole batches of cadets well before they had completed the course. For instance, in December 1883 instructions were received that the top twenty of the Junior Division, who had done one year at the College, should be commissioned immediately with the seniors. The numbers were made up by putting the top twenty infantry candidates from the recent entrance examination straight into the new Senior Division, which was due to pass out in July of the following year. Owing to the Christmas break intervening, this particular batch would in fact pass out after only five months' instruction. Then in March further instructions were received that fifty of the new senior term were to be commissioned at Easter. At the end of the same month the Governor was asked to recommend a further twenty cadets for immediate commissioning, and to review the cases of cadets who had failed their final examination the previous December. At a time when standards in the end-of-term examinations were being rigorously applied such demands obviously threw the whole syllabus and system of instruction into confusion.

ARMY CLASS OR CRAMMER

One redeeming factor was that a good deal of thought had been given to the educational standards for entry to both cadet colleges. The first hurdle for the aspiring cadet was a preliminary examination taken while at school at the age of about fifteen or sixteen. Some public schools then had Army classes to prepare boys for the 'further' Army Entrance Examination set by the Civil Service Commissioners. Cheltenham and Wellington, in particular, had established modern departments which taught the mathematics and science subjects required at Woolwich and also prepared a number of boys for entry to Sandhurst. Elsewhere, and even where there was an Army class, many boys left school to attend a crammer who specialised in pre-

91

paring them for the Army Entrance Examination. But only those who passed at the top of the list gained places. Between 1876 and 1882 there were over 2,740 candidates for entry to Woolwich, but only 715 gained places. For Sandhurst over the same period the chances were even more slender; out of 6,000 who took the examination, less than one in four passed high enough to be accepted.

Notes made by the Governor of the RMC in 1885, prior to a visit by the Board of Visitors, show the schools at which the 304 cadets had been educated and how many had also been to a crammer. These details disclose that nearly 79 per cent of the cadets' parents had considered it necessary for their sons to be specially tutored for the entrance examination, even where there was an Army class at their schools. Cadets coming from the universities (this entry ceased in 1892) numbered 27, of which 21 had been to a crammer. The sons of Army officers numbered 140, and of these, 43 were orphans, i.e. Queen's Cadets, or on reduced fees at the lowest scale.

ALL WORK AND NO PLAY

General Taylor's *aide-mémoire* continued with details of the timetable:

Reveille	6.30	Luncheon	2.00
First study	7.00–8.00	Riding	2.40–3.45
Breakfast	8.00	(two classes each hour)	
			3.45–4.45
Surgeon	8.30	Afternoon drill	3.00–3.45
Parade	9.00–10.00		
(two classes riding, except Saturday)		Gymnastics	4.00–5.00
		(Wednesdays only	5.00–6.00)
Second study	10.20–11.20	Sword exercises	6.00–7.00
Third study	11.25–12.40	Mess	8.00
Fourth study	12.40–2.00	Lights out	11.00

A further note was on the recreational activities for the summer term. 'The annual sports were held as usual in May, and there is cricket, racquets and lawn tennis, which are considered adequate.' With such a timetable and at most two cricket pitches and few courts, one wonders how many cadets were able to play these games regularly.

The last 'Duke's Day' at the RMC, 1885.

THE RIFLE CLUB

One activity was not mentioned – rifle shooting, for which there was the newly formed Rifle Club set up by Captain H.E.C. Kitchener, DCLI, the brother of the Sirdar Lord Kitchener of Khartoum. The extra-duty pay of the armourer sergeant and the cost of ammunition, to supplement the very inadequate issue of twenty rounds per cadet, had to be met by subscriptions; but the popularity of the club increased year by year. There was, however, some question about the safety of the ranges. After they had been inspected by a staff officer from Aldershot the Governor was asked to make several improvements. He had to reply that, as the ranges had never been officially recognised, there was no official grant for their maintenance and he had no College funds to spare. The matter was then referred to the Field Marshal, who seems to have missed the point. His reply merely indicated that he had no objection to College funds being used, and as the ranges were private he did not see why he had been involved!

Meanwhile Captain Kitchener had come under the spotlight for having carried out some experiments and damaged two rifles. This excessive zeal resulted in his being officially reprimanded by the War Office 'for committing a serious irregularity in altering and experimenting with service equipment without authority'.

A few years later a schoolboy at Harrow was writing to his father. He was aged fifteen and a half and referred to the visit of a friend some three years older than himself who was entering the Army through the Militia.

Harrow is all right for a Preliminary Examination but 6 months and James or any other crammer is more to a chap than 2 years at Harrow. I should like to go in through the Militia because then you begin much earlier, which is a distinct point. It is a well-known thing that a fellow who goes through the Militia is always much more use than a Sandhurst cadet. Be that as it may, I have to pass my further if I go to Sandhurst and then pass out. While I [would] only have to pass out of the Militia!

This was in the summer of 1890, and that November young Winston Churchill sat the preliminary examination for Sandhurst. He passed in all subjects, being amongst the youngest of the twelve out of twenty-nine from his school to achieve this result.

The next hurdle was the 'further' examination where there was such stiff competition to gain a place at Woolwich or Sandhurst. The examination was set in three sections or classes. Obligatory subjects were covered by Classes I and III, while in Class II candidates could choose two subjects.

Class I	Class II	Class III
Mathematics, arithmetic algebra, Euclid, plane trigonometry	Higher mathematics	Freehand drawing
	German or French	Geometrical drawing
Latin	Greek	
French or German	English composition	
English history	Chemistry	
	Physics	
	Physical geography and geology	

Having had two shots while in the Army class at Harrow, Winston Churchill passed at his third attempt, after spending the previous four or five months at Captain James's cramming establishment. He passed ninety-fifth out of 389 candidates, just missing an infantry cadetship by eighteen marks. Lord Randolph, who had planned for his son to go into the 60th Rifles, was very disappointed. In the end the matter was resolved, as one or two candidates did not take up their places (presumably wanting to try again for Woolwich), and Gentleman Cadet Churchill entered Sandhurst on the infantry list in September 1893.

A More Practical Course

Winston Churchill joined at a time when a number of changes in the curriculum were taking place, resulting in a far wider and more practical military syllabus at the College than previously. In 1893 the course was extended by an extra term so that it lasted eighteen months instead of a year. In *My Early Life* Sir Winston recorded that the subjects he studied were tactics, fortification, topography (i.e. map-reading), military law and military administration, and that these formed the whole curriculum. In addition there was drill, gymnastics and riding. The result of the extension of the course was to make extra time available for the study of fortification and to increase generally the practical work that was carried out in this subject. In fact, a third of the time allotted was devoted to outdoor practical work. In addition, the number of hours devoted to riding was increased as far as the means were available. A further change, already implemented, was that the cadets now fired the recruits' musketry course.

We find that in the following year of 1894 the eight hours' work on the daily programme was divided between five hours' study, which included practical work, and three hours' drill, riding or gymnastics.

Many of the improvements to the curriculum resulted from a report of the War Office Board of Visitors which had been issued in the summer of 1893. This recommended certain new studies, such as military history and geography, and the methods of reconnaissance on horseback, and that an extra hour a day should be devoted to study. It had also recommended that cadets should continue with the study of some of the subjects that they had taken for the entrance examination and strongly recommended the study of French or German. It is interesting to note that, while the Board was recommending the study of military history (which was not, in fact, in the syllabus until 1897), Winston Churchill had already taken steps to form his own military library.

It seems that one particular inspection by a Board of Visitors in 1893 was rather more searching than the then Governor, Lieutenant General Clive, had been expecting. The Board's investigations disclosed that the cadets had been allowed to arrange expensive entertainments which many could not afford. Some cadets were keeping horses while failing to pay their mess charges and laundry bills, and spending a good deal of their time at 'gymkhana', with hunting thrown in. Others were equally involved with a multiplicity of games and pursuits that previously had been kept at least in the background and more under control. Unfortunately, and somewhat inevitably, the standard of work had suffered, and the Board reported that the College needed a strong Governor and drastic reforms. Consequently, at about the date that Gentleman Cadet Churchill joined, a new Governor arrived to take over.

Major General C.J. East was a practical man with a good background of active service. Such changes as he made were entirely directed to seeing that the cadets learned the elements of soldiering. While he took a liberal view of games, and would not agree to stopping the cadets hunting, he made quite sure such activities did not interfere with the daily programme. But, while insisting on more practical outdoor instruction, he refused to make up the establishment of cadets by taking any who had not reached the educational standards required by the entrance examination.

One innovation was to send the seniors to camp for a few days each term, while an annual camp for the whole College was held on Barossa. This is the training area at the back of the College where so many generations of cadets have sweated and toiled on every imaginable outdoor exercise from map-reading and night compass marches to field engineering, which included digging trenches and rivetments in the stony ground; from night patrols to riding out to Lower Star Post, where the ground was deceptively flat and open but cut across with banks and hidden ditches that could prove disastrous to the unwary.

All this and the chance of getting as much extra riding as possible certainly appealed to young Churchill. In the chapter in *My Early Life* devoted to his eighteen months at Sandhurst he writes, 'At Sandhurst I had a new start', and he made the most of the opportunities it offered. He passed out in the top twenty, with 190 out of 200 marks in the final examination for riding and excellent marks for tactics and fortification. This placing was higher than any of the candidates for the Cavalry, and it was in that Arm that he now sought his commission. His recently widowed mother wrote to the Duke of Cambridge, who had recommended her son for the 60th five years previously, and with the Field Marshal's blessing Winston was transferred off the infantry list. In February 1895 he received his commission and joined the 4th Hussars in Aldershot.

THE SWORD AND OTHER PRIZES

The Victorian era saw the institution of several awards both for good conduct and distinction in studies. At Woolwich it was customary for prizes to be given in the main subjects. The grant for this, which was £50 in 1830, became £84 at the turn of the century and was sufficient to buy a number of leather-bound books or cases of instruments to be won at the half-yearly examinations. For a short period in the middle of the century the recipients of these prizes, which were not given to the practical class, wore a strip of gold lace on their collars. But at about the same time any cadet achieving exceptional results in the six main subjects, on promotion to the practical class, received a medal to be worn in uniform.

From 1836 onwards at Woolwich a Regulation Sword was presented at each commissioning to the 'best-conducted cadet'. This award for exemplary conduct was first won by C.A. Brooke, who was commissioned into the Royal Engineers. Over the years 'the Sword' almost invariably went to the Senior Under Officer, of which there was only one at the Shop.

The award for the 'most distinguished cadet of the commission class' was the Pollock Medal. This prize was instituted at Addiscombe in 1848 and continued to be awarded at the RMA from 1861 onwards. The award commemorated the career of Field Marshal Sir George Pollock, Bt, GCB, KCSI, who had been at the Shop from 1801 to 1803, before joining the

Sketch mapping on Barossa in 1893 – 'The Start'. RMA Sandhurst Collection.

Bengal Artillery in the East India Company's service. In 1842, during the First Afghan War, Pollock was given an Army command, and thus became the first British artillery officer to hold such an appointment. On the occasion that the Pollock was first awarded at Woolwich it was won by T. Fraser, who also received the Sword.

The memory of another Addiscombe cadet who had served with the Bengal Artillery, Major General Sir Henry Tombs, VC, KCB, was also commemorated at the Shop. Tombs had served for thirty years in India with great distinction and had won the Victoria Cross attempting to save the life of a brother officer during the siege of Delhi. The Tombs Prize was awarded to the senior artillery cadet of his batch. Instituted in 1877, it was first won by F.E.D. Acland.

During the period up to 1900 the same individuals won the Sword and the Pollock on twenty-nine occasions. Any other combinations were extremely rare. In 1893 W.C. Symon won all three of these major awards, and in 1900 F.A. Finis, the winner of the Tombs, was also awarded the Sword.

An award common to both colleges was instituted by command of Queen Victoria in 1897, the year of Her Majesty's Diamond Jubilee. This was the Queen Victoria Medal. At Sandhurst this medal, the personal gift of the Sovereign, was always awarded to the cadet highest in the order of merit on passing out. The first winner was J.F. Freeland, who was commissioned into the 35th Sikh Infantry. At Woolwich, however, such conditions were somewhat in conflict with those of existing and long-established prizes, so it was decreed that the Queen's Medal should become the prize for 'proficiency in military subjects of study'. The first Shop cadet to win the award was C.M. Wagstaff. Two years later the award went to C.C. Trench, whose general conduct and excellence at his studies had also won him the Sword and the Pollock Medal.

At the RMC the first award of the Sword of Honour was made in 1890 to H.G.M. Amos, who was commissioned into the West India Regiment. Correspondence in 1896 shows the relationship between the Sword of Honour, always regarded as the major award at the College, and other prizes. The Director General of Military Education, who seems to have been inadequately briefed, had written to the Governor:

When Lieut.-Colonel the Hon. A.H.A. Anson, VC, died in 1877, his comrades and friends with the sanction of HRH and the Secretary of State for War instituted the Anson Memorial Sword to be presented to the most deserving cadet of his term at the Royal Military College. The money subscribed was invested in trustees who were to hand over the accruing interest to the Governor. It would appear that the Anson Memorial Sword has practically ceased to exist.

Major General East felt it necessary to put the record straight and replied in some detail:

The Anson Memorial Sword has not ceased to exist, it having since its institution been presented once a year to the cadet . . . who passes first out of the College at Christmas. At midsummer a sword is given to the cadet passing out first, out of the annual sum allowed for prizes, and is known as the General Proficiency Sword. The Sword of Honour referred to in para. 22 of Standing Orders is awarded at the end of each term to the under officer who is considered to have had the best influence amongst the cadets generally, and to have exerted himself most successfully in maintaining discipline in his position as an under officer. In fact to the most deserving cadet, although not necessarily passing out high.

The following year the Queen's Medal was instituted and the Governor had to change the conditions for the award of the Anson Sword, which was subsequently given to the cadet who was runner-up for the Sword of Honour in the summer term. The first recorded winner of the Anson Sword was F.S. Maude, who joined the Coldstream Guards in 1883.

Before leaving this survey of the major prizes, let us look at two statistics for the period ending in 1900. At the RMA there had been 138 recipients of the Sword; of these, 100 joined the Royal Engineers. At the RMC, of the first ten winners of the Queen's Medal, seven went into the Indian Army, and four of these joined the 35th Sikh Infantry.

THE BOER WAR

Major General East carried through the promised reforms at Sandhurst with a firm hand. As a result of his success he was promoted and made a Knight Commander of the Bath. Some of the changes he instituted have already been mentioned: more practical work and tactical exercises, together with the introduction of military history. Languages were again taught, and with the extra six months, more time was given to tactics, law and military administration. The vacations were shortened and the daily programme was reorganised to allow for three hours of drill, riding or gymnastics, and five hours' study, which included either French or German. Such was the situation when Lieutenant General Sir E. Markham, KCB, took over early in 1899. But by October the country was at war and the new Governor had to face problems of a very different nature.

At Sandhurst the impact of the Boer War came almost overnight. Any cadet who had done two terms was commissioned immediately. Officers on the staff were recalled to their regiments. Replacements were hardly in the saddle before they were again posted. The Infantry Detachment now came from a nearby Militia battalion, or a newly formed Reserve Unit, and the Governor was constantly complaining of their behaviour. In one letter to

99

the Deputy Adjutant General, Aldershot, he wrote, 'They have been drunk about ever since they came here. Most of them are in the Guard Room now, and those who are not are hardly able to walk.'

Meanwhile the course had to be shortened. Some recently introduced subjects were cut back or dropped. The time allocated for language instruction was reduced by two thirds. As the demand for officers increased, a complete batch of intermediates was commissioned with the seniors. Juniors became seniors within weeks, and the whole sequence of instruction went haywire. In midsummer 1900 there were 125 seniors and 236 juniors, the latter having arrived in January. To make up the number to be commissioned the top sixty juniors were passed out on their first term's examination results after only six months.

At this very moment the War Office was announcing guide lines for a revised course. On paper the proposals were impressive: an eighteen-month course, more practical work and better instructors, the majority of whom should have qualified at the Staff College. Meanwhile the Governor was desperately trying to adjust the syllabus for an absolute maximum of two terms. 'Machine-guns' and 'Zones of Penetration' appear as explanatory lectures under the heading 'Military Engineering'; patrolling, scouting and reconnaissance were to be taught as part of tactics, while voluntary subjects were detailed as ambulance and stretcher drill, alongside first aid, range-finding and signalling. Much of this planning, however, had to be temporarily abandoned, for by May 1901 the only cadets left at the RMC were 178 juniors who had joined three months previously.

At the RMA on the outbreak of war there were similar demands for early commissioning, but somehow the flow of cadets through the Academy was better controlled. Within two months both the top classes had passed out, 140 to the Royal Artillery and 56 to the Royal Engineers. In January 1900 a double intake of 'snookers' arrived and the course was reduced to twelve months. This pattern was maintained, and by the autumn of 1901 the number of cadets under instruction had reached 306, the highest in the history of the Academy. As at the RMC, the constant changes of instructors created difficulties, but by shortening the vacations a modified syllabus could be completed in twelve to fifteen months. For the cadets there was little let-up. Reveille was at 6.15 a.m. and rollcall at 10 p.m., with lights out half an hour later. The first study started at 8.15 a.m., and the last study ended at 7.15 p.m. Interspersed, apart from time for meals, were two hours' drill and an hour for games, which defaulters spent on the Square.

CHAPTER 8

A Pattern Emerges

DIRECTIVE FOR A NEW ERA

The death of Queen Victoria in January 1901 came as a shock to the whole nation. Less than a year before, she had travelled down to Woolwich to visit the wounded soldiers from South Africa in the Herbert Hospital. The Cadet Company had mounted a guard of honour and lined part of the road near the hospital. From there she had driven on to see the Prince Imperial's statue on the edge of the recreation ground, where a special stand had been erected for the benefit of the staff and their families. Some of the cadets present on that occasion, notable for its informality, now paraded with the 200-strong contingent from the Academy who lined part of the route of the Queen's funeral procession along the Mall. Opposite were the Sandhurst cadets. This was a very different occasion, one of pomp and solemnity, the nation's tribute to a great queen, a day that marked the passing of an era.

The depth of public concern over the disasters suffered by the Army in the early days of the war is mirrored in the near hysteria that swept through the country at the time of the relief of Ladysmith and of Mafeking. Moreover no quick remedy had followed, and with the war dragging on for another two years, official inquiries into the causes of the early failures were got under way. One of these was a Government Committee on the Education and Training of Officers of the Army, presided over by the Right Honourable A. Akers-Douglas, MP. The remaining members were two other MPs, two headmasters (Eton and St Paul's) and three serving officers, one of whom later resigned on being appointed Governor of the RMA. Seventy-three witnesses gave evidence, including the Commander-in-Chief, and a questionnaire was sent to commanding officers throughout the Army.

After a year's work the report was published – two months before the official ending of the war in the spring of 1902. The Committee had been given very wide terms of reference, in fact they had started at square one. What changes were required, if any, to improve the system of training candidates for the Army at the public schools and universities? Should the cadet colleges be retained? If so, were any changes needed?

EDUCATIONAL STANDARDS

The report opens with some general comments on military education in the Army, such as 'Economy appears to have been sought without sufficient regard to efficiency'. The Committee also felt that an increasing amount of money was being spent on elementary education of a general nature at the expense of much needed technical military education. There was ample evidence of 'widespread dissatisfaction with the present state of education, both military and general, among officers of the Army as a class', and this clearly indicated that the early education of young officers was not on proper lines.

During their deliberations the Committee had come to the conclusion that the cadet colleges were needed, as being the only means of providing an immediate reserve of young officers in time of war. Moreover it was recognised that the Militia alone could not meet the annual requirement of 800 officers. Furthermore, a large majority of commanding officers had declared a preference for the Sandhurst/Woolwich product, and this particularly applied to the technical Arms. The advantage of cadets having acquired habits of discipline and obedience to orders was a further factor in reaching this decision.

The Committee then dealt with what they described as 'the antecedent education of Army candidates'. This they considered should be of a general nature and controlled by the entrance examination, but here changes were needed to ensure that candidates were well grounded. A new examination was required, concentrating on basic subjects representing a good general education. The changes recommended were: fewer papers but firmer direction through compulsory subjects; the introduction of either French or German as a compulsory foreign-language qualification; greater emphasis on mathematics for entry to Woolwich. Also, there should now be one examination instead of separate ones for Woolwich, Sandhurst and the Militia. Furthermore, Militia (and Yeomanry) officers wishing to obtain commissions in the Army would have to qualify at the entrance examination, and then take a competitive examination in military subjects similar to the passing-out examination for cadets.

COLLEGE REFORMS

Turning to the cadet colleges, the Committee felt that the age for entry should be standardised at between seventeen and nineteen. The RMA came in for few comments. The cadets' rooms were overcrowded; there

Captain F.G. Guggisberg and his Fortification Class at the RMA in 1901.

should be a chapel and a resident chaplain; also a riding school and covered drill shed. So far the path was well worn and predictable. Regarding the syllabus, they considered that the teaching of tactics and military history had been utterly neglected. Also, the cadets should have a month or six weeks in camp on Salisbury Plain, during which time they should go to Shoeburyness for two weeks' gunnery practice.

In contrast the report on the RMC was far from favourable. The cadets spent too much time indoors; there was too little supervision and little or no inducement to work; and it was apparent that the amount of drill was excessive. On the subject of military training, 'the Committee were surprised to learn that the cadets are not instructed in either musketry or revolver shooting at Sandhurst, though range accommodation is available in the immediate neighbourhood, and they were still more surprised to learn that such cadets as were able to find time to shoot have to join a club and pay a subscription of £1 a term'.

Regarding the course of studies at the RMC, there was a lack of balance and subjects were taught in watertight compartments. It was quite indefensible that within the existing year's course only sixty hours were devoted to tactics and that more than half of this time was spent indoors. Moreover the subject was allocated only 450 marks out of 3,800 in the final examination. All this and much more the Committee argued must be put right. There should be more tactics and military history. The study of military topography, engineering and tactics must be co-ordinated, and practical work in the field should lead up to tactical schemes. Similarly, examinations should be practical as far as possible. A summer camp with manoeuvres and field training was also needed. Musketry should be taught at Sandhurst as an essential part of the cadet's training, rather than young officers having to be sent to the School of Musketry immediately they were commissioned.

Before any cadet was commissioned he should pass out in riding, musketry and revolver. All cadets should be taught signalling and cavalry cadets should receive instruction in the elements of the veterinary service. Cadets going into the Indian Army should learn Hindustani. As at the RMA, instruction in the French or German languages, being covered by the entrance examination, would be omitted from the syllabus. To achieve proper standards on these lines the Committee recommended that the course at Sandhurst should last two years. Furthermore, the impression amongst officers appointed as instructors that they had been 'put on the shelf' must be corrected. The tour of duty should not exceed four years, and inducements should include subsequent accelerated promotion or nomination to the Staff College.

How Many Cadets?

On the question of numbers, the Committee considered that Woolwich, with a capacity of 300 and a two-year course, could meet the needs of the Royal Artillery and Royal Engineers. The problem was to meet the requirement for young officers in the remainder of the Army. With an eighteen-month course and the present accommodation, Sandhurst could not provide even half of the numbers required annually. Moreover the Committee were strongly recommending a two-year course. This meant that the cadet establishment would have to be raised on both counts. The figure proposed was 650, and this recommendation should be implemented 'as soon as circumstances permitted', a tactful way of saying 'as soon as the cost of the extra accommodation and staff could be authorised'.

The remainder of the report dealt with university candidates (there was a cautious move towards offering up to a hundred commissions a year) and the 'subsequent military education' of all Army officers. But here we must leave this fascinating report, itself a study of problems that had been brought into sharp focus by war – the last of the 'Gentlemen's Wars' – eighty years ago.

HALDANE ACTS

Some of the proposed changes were delayed for lack of funds, others were abandoned as the storm-clouds gathered. While the ending of the Boer War brought the opportunity for the Army to reorganise and retrain, it was only after the appointment of Mr Haldane as Secretary of State for War in 1905 (a position he held until 1912) that the Government could be persuaded to approve and finance any major reforms. What Viscount Haldane, as he was to become, achieved may be judged by some comparisons between the Army of 1905 and that of 1911. In 1905 the Yeomanry and Volunteers had no field artillery, engineers, transport or medical services. The Militia were not available to serve outside the United Kingdom. Excluding the troops in India and the colonies, the Army could only produce three Regular Divisions and a Cavalry Division of three brigades for service overseas. In 1911, however, Britain had a Territorial Force organised in divisions with all ancillary services. The Army Reserve had been considerably increased and the Militia had become a Special Reserve available to maintain an Expeditionary Force, while the Regular Army had six Divisions (with a seventh available within six weeks) and a Cavalry Division of five brigades.

These remarkable results had in fact been achieved without any increase in the numbers involved. The total strength of the Regular Army in the United Kingdom with its reserves, together with the Territorial Force, was now 717,326. This was over 18,000 less than the Army and various Militia and Volunteer units mustered in 1905. But the training of the reserves and the creation and training of the Territorial Divisions needed large numbers of regular officers, and this in turn brought further pressure on the cadet colleges.

THE SHOP INVADED

It is plain that in the first decade of the twentieth century many influences were at work: the need to adjust to peace conditions and economies; the move to improve the quality of the officer corps; the reorganisation of the Army itself under Haldane in the face of the growing threat of a major war. Overall a pattern emerges; yet as a stream fills from the dykes and ditches, itself to feed the river below, so pools and eddies form and the pace of flow seems never constant. As far as Woolwich was concerned there was a good deal of ebb and flow. The two-year course was reinstated in 1902. Military history, interior economy and military law were introduced for the first time, together with signalling and the use of the field telephone. Owing to the legacy of wartime expansion, however, there were blocks in promotion, and the number of cadets accepted for the Shop was reduced.

As there was soon accommodation to spare and Sandhurst was over-flowing, a Sandhurst Company was taken in as lodgers. This invasion began in the summer of 1905 and continued with one brief gap until December 1911, by which time additional accommodation at Sandhurst had been built. Meanwhile the normal admissions to the Shop had dropped to around seventy a year. The Sandhurst Company was sixty strong and organised as No. 4 Company. They had their own officers and course of instruction, and in review order they wore their distinctive red tunics; but in all other respects they were an integral part of the Shop and were commanded by an under officer of the senior class.

BIG GUNS AND MOUNTING PRESSURES

A cadet of 1908 looks back on the period of the Haldane reforms:

There was no need [in those days] to advertise for officers, or offer them degrees to tempt them into the Army. For the Shop, especially, there was stiff com-petition for the thirty-five or so places available twice a year, and once in the Army, an officer intended to spend his life there. So the curriculum was solely designed to produce Army officers, with no thought of preparing them for other careers in later life. In 1908–09 there was no definite orientation against Germany. The German menace did not really appear to ordinary people till Agadir in 1911. My term at the Shop passed out after eighteen months, instead of two years, because there was a sudden shortage of officers for some reason. The syllabus of training included 'square-bashing', gun drill, gym, riding, ordnance, field engineering, including bridging, 'scotch-up', military history, with maths and French as the only non-military subjects. There was plenty of 'spit and polish' and meticulous cleanliness for Sunday church parade. . . . Incidentally, 'scotch-up' was the art, necessary for coast defence guns in those days, of moving pieces of ordnance with the aid of gins, rollers and levers. There were several old cannon lying about the Shop which we used to move from place to place.

Apart from the Sandhurst Company the two intakes of 1908 only totalled 72, and as we have seen the course was suddenly reduced to three terms. Then in July 1909 two classes were commissioned together to meet the demands of the additional field artillery regiments which were forming. The following spring 74 cadets were accepted without examination and on nomination alone – an unprecedented step – and over the year 110 cadets were commissioned into the Royal Artillery and 31 into the Royal Engineers. Early in 1912 a double intake joined, filling the accommodation vacated by the Sandhurst cadets, and the course reverted to the normal two years. By now the reorganisation of the Royal Field Artillery had been completed, but the pressure was mounting from other quarters and every place had to be kept filled.

On New Year's Day 1908 an announcement that tenders were being sought for the construction of new accommodation blocks at the RMC drew an immediate protest from the Commandant, who had been kept very much in the dark. Although the Akers-Douglas Committee had spelt out the requirement five years previously, the money had still not been voted and it was another eighteen months before the decision to start building was made public. Some, but not many, of the other recommendations had meanwhile been implemented.

Lieutenant General Markham, the last to hold the dual appointment of Governor and Commandant, had been replaced by the younger Colonel G.C. Kitson in the autumn of 1902. Kitson had previously been Commandant of the RMC, Kingston, in Canada. Unlike his predecessor at Sandhurst, whose last months in office had been marred by a series of unexplained fires in the company lines and a serious disturbance in Camberley involving a large number of cadets during a fête at the Foresters Inn, Colonel Kitson kept a firm grip on both discipline and administration right from the start. No department was spared the rigours of his inspections. Irregularities in the use of College funds, inferior messing arrangements, poorly prepared lectures – all came in for censure and correction. Nor did the new Commandant hesitate to press the War Office on many long overdue changes and improvements. A Sub-Post and Telegraph Office was established in the Buglers' Room at the Grand Entrance. A permanent instructor in Hindustani was appointed. Extra musicians were recruited for the band. Funds were obtained so that signalling instruction could be started, £300 for equipment and extra duty pay for an officer as superintendent (£50 per annum) and two sergeants at 1s. 9d. a day while the cadets were in residence.

The purchase of a printing press also dates from this period. When an Army order forbade the use of local printers, in favour of the work being sent to the Stationery Office, Kitson declared that he was not prepared to wait six months for instructional pamphlets to be delivered. He had the necessary money in the Instrument Fund, the Royal Engineers detachment already operated a small press and could always find a printer within their own establishment, and the Accountant supported his case. War Office approval came within weeks, and the press, which then cost a little over £100, has been in use ever since.

In May 1903 Kitson warned the County Surveyor of the pending increase in numbers. He gave the existing strength as: 36 officers, 50 servants, 80 others (who presumably included families), and an establishment of 360 gentlemen cadets which would increase to 640. His half-yearly report at the end of the summer term shows the same confident note but with significant reservations. Discipline had been maintained and rifle shooting had improved. The company system instituted at the beginning of the year had proved an entire success. The Cadet Sergeant Major, Colour Sergeants and NCOs were especially worthy of praise. The camp on Salisbury Plain had given the gentlemen cadets a good deal of practical knowledge, but in such a short course this month spent solely on practical work had been at the expense of certain subjects, such as the study of topography (part of military history) and in particular field sketching. With a two-year course these difficulties would be overcome.

PROGRESS UNDER DIFFICULTIES

The two-year course was brought in the following January, but only one batch completed the full course. There was a sudden demand for officers in the spring of 1905, and orders came for the course to be temporarily reduced to one year. Furthermore, all cadets who had been in residence for a complete year were to be passed out at the end of the term if qualified by examination. Their places were quickly filled and, as already mentioned, the overflow was sent off to Woolwich as the Sandhurst Company.

The Commandant did not hesitate to underline his difficulties in his next report, from which the following are extracts:

The health of the College very good but the sanitary conditions utterly out of date. The recommendations of Sir Henry Hildyard's Committee had not been

RMC transport on the march to summer camp on Salisbury Plain in 1903.

carried out, and it was strongly urged that before a penny was spent on the new buildings, a very large sum should be expended on the necessary improvements in the College. If good work was to be expected of the cadets they should not be three in a room with no proper baths, out-of-date sanitary arrangements, and the basement full of women and children. The return to a one year's course – just as the first two-year men graduated – was not conducive to the efficiency of the College.

Soon the course was extended, but only by six months. A revised syllabus dated 1907 shows that the tactics course had been considerably extended to take account of the magazine rifle and quick-firing artillery, as well as co-operation between Arms and night operations. Language instruction had been increased, and the cadets were put through the Trained Soldier's Musketry Course. Signalling, no longer a voluntary subject, included test messages by flag in Morse as well as semaphore, while unit administration and sanitation had been added. Military engineering and topography were now to be taught from the official manuals, with plenty of practical work. On the other hand, military history was still only concerned with the Peninsular and Waterloo campaigns.

FINANCIAL PLOYS

The Commandant of those days was still constantly beset with the problems of financing any change or improvement he was trying to make. This may be illustrated by the appointment in 1907 of a Mr E.S. Taylor in the new post of mess secretary. Colonel Kitson's earlier efforts to improve the messing arrangements eventually resulted in the War Office agreeing to set up a committee to consider the proposals in detail. These included the

appointment of a 'mess manager' at a proper salary. The post was sanctioned, but only providing there was no charge to the State, over and above the figure of £150, plus £50 in lieu of quarters, already covered by the College annual grant. To find a suitable man Kitson decided to offer £500 a year (rising by annual increments to £700), finding the balance from College funds. Incidentally this salary was more than the professor in German received.

On a rather different level was the matter of the officers' library. In his last year of office Kitson was able to close a file which had been opened fifteen years previously, when a request to the War Office to buy a work entitled *History of the British Army 1660–1700* was turned down 'as no funds are available for works of this description'. Arguments as to the need for an officers' library of books of a professional character had been bandied to and fro ever since, and it is much to the credit of the Colonel that a War Office grant of £50 a year was finally agreed.

Early in 1908 Colonel Capper was told to pass out double the normal numbers in the summer and once again reduce the course to a year. His protest at having to accept 230 replacements the same autumn, thereby throwing the whole programme out of phase, was swept to one side, the official reply being that fifty candidates would be lost to the Service for six months, together with their fees over the same period. Whatever the Treasury view concerning the lost fees, which anyway would have been totally absorbed in maintaining the extra numbers, it is clear that the

Church Parade at the RMC in 1905. Note the entrance in use before the Chapel was enlarged.

Government was determined to carry through the Haldane reforms – in this instance to cover the formation of the Special Reserve. Nevertheless the Commandant and his staff must have been heartily sick of having to 'break into double time' every year or so.

Soon work was to start on the new accommodation blocks, and we find the Commandant giving permission for a light horse tramway to be built from Blackwater Station to the site. The track ran behind the Old Buildings and ended at a turntable inside the brick-built contractor's shed that was erected behind the gymnasium. In later years this same building, once emptied of the tools and piles of building material, has served many purposes: drill shed, emergency accommodation at times of mobilisation, bicycle shed, miniature range, cinema, lecture hall, model room, book store, and now a 'temporary' extension to the Library that itself is established in the former gymnasium. In many ways this reflects the story of Sandhurst as a whole, where over the years temporary buildings have become permanent and permanent buildings have often been adapted to other uses, to keep pace with the evolutionary process that itself is subjected to external pressures and the vagaries of the planners.

HIS MAJESTY'S DISPLEASURE

Colonel Capper, who like his immediate predecessors was under pressure to commission more officers in less time, and could hardly have been in ignorance of the requirement to provide for 650 cadets under instruction, must have been somewhat taken aback when he was asked if he wished to retain any of the Old Buildings once the new accommodation for 420 cadets was ready for occupation. In his reply to the War Office he pointed out that the New Buildings would provide only for six companies of gentlemen cadets and a few bachelor officers, which left nothing for the extra cadets, or indeed offices, storerooms, clerks, armoury and sergeants' mess, let alone quarters and accommodation for the housekeeper and married families. The nub of the matter is disclosed in his next comment which deals with a proposal to save money by transferring furniture from the Old to the New Buildings.

I would note that to remove the present archaic furniture over would in my opinion be useless. It costs £150 per annum, fair wear and tear, to keep it on its legs, i.e. with personal damage item, roughly 10/– per cadet, and the general poverty of the whole outfit was seriously commented upon by Their Majesties at their visit in July. It is very indifferent stuff, that would hardly find harbour in rooms occupied by under-servants in private families. His Majesty was not pleased with the 'barrack-room' tables which form the outfit of the Halls of Study, and advocated sloping desks of modern educational pattern.

111

CHAPTER 9

For King, Country and Freedom

PUBLIC DUTIES

At the funeral of King Edward VII in May 1910 the Sandhurst cadets lining the route had been given a privileged position in Horse Guards Avenue. Behind them were the Cavalry and opposite was the Woolwich contingent. Two months later King George V, accompanied by Queen Mary and HRH Field Marshal the Duke of Connaught and his Duchess, visited the Royal Military College, the first of a number of occasions when the King was to show a personal interest in the life and work of the two cadet colleges. At the coronation of Their Majesties the following June the Shop and RMC contingents were formed up opposite each other at the entrance to the Abbey itself and alongside the Dartmouth cadets, a place of honour indeed. Major Waite, the riding master, was in charge of the horseholders at Westminster, and a note in the College records shows that the Coronation Medal was issued to the Commandant, the senior Cadet Colour Sergeant and the winner of the Sword of Honour. Subsequently the Second in Command (Lieutenant Colonel Hickman), Major Waite and Regimental Sergeant Major Payne were awarded the medal on the Commandant's representation that the cadet battalion should be treated in the same way as an infantry battalion.

THE CHAMPION COMPANY

At the half-yearly inspection in July Colonel Capper concluded his report with the following announcement:

With a view to affording all ranks in a company an opportunity of combining to give practical effect to that spirit of company *esprit de corps* which has always formed such an important factor in the efficiency of the Royal Military College, I have instituted a stystem of awarding marks to the best company in certain military and athletic exercises, the company gaining the highest total number of marks to be styled 'The Champion Company at Arms' and to have the honour of becoming the right flank company of the cadet battalion during the ensuing term. The competition has been so arranged that whilst double marks are awarded for all collective military exercises, as compared with athletics, individuals who have excelled in the latter earn also a certain number of marks for their companies.

NEW BUILDINGS COMPLETED

That September the return of the cadets for the winter term was delayed for a week owing to a railway strike and 'unrest in the labour market', which had held up the delivery of essential materials for the completion of the New Buildings. A cadet who joined in 1911 recalls:

I was there from September 1911 to July 1912, a short course for the time being, because, I imagine, of a shortage of infantry officers. Half of the 'New' Buildings was then finished and we were one of the three companies that moved over from the Old Buildings. I was in 'E', and oddly enough when I commanded No. 3 Company in 1933–34 they were in the same block that I had been in about twenty years earlier! Halfway through our first term the other companies moved from the Old Buildings into the west wing of the 'New'. . . . The training was pretty elementary. Much drill, PT, riding, signalling (semaphore only) and sketching. Somewhat primitive tactics and military engineering (the last named almost Crimean, dealing largely in fascines and gabions). Indoors, Wellington's campaigns, military law, and either French, German or Urdu.

For the first time for a hundred years there were no cadets in the Old Buildings, and within a few days the long-awaited modernisation of the interior was in the hands of contractors. At this point Colonel Capper handed over to Colonel L.A.M. Stopford, and to both of these Commandants the College owes a great deal.

The year 1912 saw the return of the Sandhurst Company from Woolwich, bring the numbers up to 420, and in September the eighteen-month course was reinstated. A hundred of the senior term, who were at the bottom of the list in the end-of-term examinations, were kept back for another six months and an extra company was formed. As the reconstructed quarters in the Old Buildings were not ready, the new 'G' Company went under canvas for the first few weeks of term. That summer the last of the annual camps on Salisbury Plain was held. The pressure was on, and with a planned establishment of 700 cadets, more staff would soon be needed.

A cadet in the last Sandhurst Company at the Shop tells of his experiences:

For the first few weeks we drilled in plain clothes, then we were measured for our uniforms by Davis and Co. Both the service dress and blues had stand-up collars and three-stud white collars inside. I was in 'E' House, in a room with four others. The Shop cadets so monopolised the few rusty baths that we were lucky to

113

get one in before dinner, and our mess room was in a hut. On lunch parade, woe betide anyone who had neglected to put on a fresh white collar, and the under officer could detect at once if our buttons had not been cleaned a few minutes before. If you were given a 'Hoxter' [a punishment parade] the worst part was having to do rifle drill in leather gloves.

Amongst the Shop cadets there was a good deal of ragging – mostly dowsing in the fountain, or chasing along the 'streets' inside the precincts. By comparison the New Buildings at Sandhurst were infinitely more comfortable and there was much less ragging. I felt that the seniors monopolised the sports facilities, which were scanty. I only remember playing a little tennis and cricket that summer and occasionally hiring a horse, but we played a lot of bicycle polo on the Square. Looking back, I don't think we were told enough about regimental life, or the lessons of recent wars, such as the use of barbed wire and hand grenades, although we did have a demonstration on explosives.

'Scotch-up.' Practical instruction at the RMA in 1912.

SPORT

While the RMC was struggling with the problems of expansion, the RMA had been kept on a more even keel, and with the departure of the Sandhurst Company and arrival of a double intake, as already mentioned, the normal two-year course was quickly reinstated. Opportunities for sport at this date probably favoured the Woolwich cadets as at Sandhurst there were no sports grounds to cater for the considerably increased numbers. Of Woolwich, in the years just prior to the Great War, Maurice-Jones writes:

From 1900 onwards games began to play an ever-increasing part in the life of the gentleman cadet. Athletic sports, cricket, Rugby, soccer, racquets, gymnastics, aquatic sports, fencing and revolver shooting had for some time been included in the recreations of the cadet. During the period under consideration, hockey, rifle shooting, boxing and lawn tennis were added.

The main object of each 'first team' was to defeat Sandhurst, but there were opportunities for everyone, with inter-company competitions and weekend leave to play for Old Boys' sides or to play golf, sail or ride. The annual fixtures between the two colleges were for athletics, cricket, Rugby, soccer, hockey and revolver shooting, together with racquets, gymnastics and fencing. Adding up the wins and losses in the inter-collegiate matches between 1900 and 1914, we find that generally speaking Sandhurst had the stronger teams in cricket, soccer and racquets, the Shop could claim to have the edge when it came to Rugby, hockey and revolver shooting, and otherwise the two were evenly matched. For a number of years cadets had competed at fencing in the Royal Naval and Military Tournament, but in 1910 a special event was introduced for teams (in foil, sabre, and bayonet) from Woolwich and Sandhurst to compete against each other.

Now, more than ever before, the two cadets colleges were in the public eye. Many public schools maintained strong cadet corps and vied with each other to produce candidates. In 1913 nearly half the cadets at the RMA came from six schools, headed by Wellington (38) and Cheltenham (34), and backed up by Clifton, Marlborough, Winchester, all of which produced cadets in double figures.

ROYAL OCCASIONS AND NEW COLOURS

In April King George V, with Queen Mary and the Princess Mary, visited the Shop. In *The Shop Story* Colonel Maurice-Jones describes the occasion as follows:

The cadets were formed up as a battalion in line under the command of Major E.S. Hoare Nairne, RA. The band of the Royal Artillery was on the ground, and the battalion received His Majesty with a Royal Salute. Then they marched past in column and returned in quarter-column, reforming in line. Afterwards the cadets brought on their field guns at the double and went through the drill, everything being done with precision and smartness.

Two months later His Majesty, accompanied by the Queen and the Princesses Mary and Victoria, presented new Colours to the RMC. After the trooping and march-past, Their Majesties inspected the reconstructed accommodation in the Old Buildings, before, as reported in the *Morning Post*, 'proceeding to the New College, where they inspected the kitchens, the dining hall, anterooms, and sleeping rooms of the cadets, and asked many questions as to the feeding of the cadets, and were also shown the menus for the whole of the week'. The old Colours were later laid up in the Chapel during a church parade attended by Lord Roberts.

The half-yearly inspection that summer was carried out by the Chief of the Imperial General Staff, Field Marshal Sir John French. In his address he paid tribute to the steady progress that had been made and referred to the introduction of an extra term, reminding the cadets that on joining their regiments their role would be 'to train and instruct their men in peace and lead them in war, and the longer the preparation they had for it, the better they would be able to carry out that great work'.

The three-term course was basically the same as that introduced five years previously. The most important change was that tactics, field engineering, map-reading and field sketching were taught concurrently and marked throughout the whole eighteen months, with a final examination out of doors lasting two days, plus two three-hour written papers. Hygiene was introduced as an additional subject, and cadets who took both French and German could gain extra marks.

THE SHOP 1914–1918
When mobilisation came in August 1914 the Shop was on summer vacation. A senior term had just been commissioned, and the staff and remaining cadets were scattered all over the British Isles and most of Europe. Of those in the latter, one of the French lecturers and four cadets failed to get out of Germany in time and were interned. The new senior class was commissioned immediately, followed by another class two months later. Meanwhile the number of 'snookers' to be admitted in September had been nearly doubled, and the Civil Service Commissioners announced that two further examinations would be held that autumn, and that subsequently there would be four entrance examinations a year. The payment of fees was set aside for the duration of the war and the age for

Major General Sir Lintorn Simmons, Governor RMA Woolwich 1869–75.
From a painting by Gentleman Cadet L.G. Fawkes.
Royal Artillery Institution.

The presentation of the King George V Banner by His Majesty, in the presence of Queen Mary, Princess Mary and Field Marshal The Duke of Connaught, at Buckingham Palace on 7 November 1918. RMA Sandhurst Collection.

entry changed to between sixteen and a half and twenty-five. Now there would be no vacations and little or no time for games, and the course would be reduced to six months.

After two weeks' recruit training on the Square (in suits and bowler hats until the service dress uniforms were fitted), those destined for the Gunners, both Field and Garrison, or the Engineers had separate training syllabuses. The instruction in each case was confined to strictly military subjects. For instance, the syllabus for a Royal Field Artillery cadet comprised: artillery training, tactics, administration, map-reading, riding, together with workshops, drill, signalling and PT, with just a modicum of horse-management, slide rule and hygiene thrown in.

By the end of 1914 the number of cadets under instruction had risen to 323, and over the whole year 267 had been commissioned. In October the last batch of pre-war entry was inspected by His Majesty, who presented the Sword of Honour to Senior Under Officer E.E. Nott-Bower. This award was made whenever a batch was passing out, but the other awards and prizes continued to be given twice a year. One of the recipients of the Pollock Gold Medal in 1916 was R.W.P. Yates, who had been educated at Bedford School. Yates had the distinction of being the first Shop cadet who had ever obtained full marks in any subject at the Army Entrance Examination. This was in chemistry and physics, where he was awarded the full 2,000 marks. In fact he nearly scored a double, as in the higher mathematics paper he scored 1,990 marks, having had 10 marks deducted for spelling 'parallel' wrongly!

For the first two years of the war the Shop was committed to turning out 500 regular officers each year. Then as the officer cadet schools began to function some of the pressure was eased, particularly as the War Office had begun to doubt the wisdom of continuing with the short six-month course at the RMA. There was no shortage of candidates to take the entrance examination, and in spite of the extension of the course to nine months in 1916, some 300 cadets were commissioned from Woolwich over the following year. Judging, however, by the results of the recently reintroduced passing-out examinations, the problem was not that of numbers but how to maintain the quality. In June 1917 the length of the course was again increased, making it a year in all, but the number of cadets who had to be removed or dropped a term was now 10 per cent, and within a year this figure had doubled.

W.F. Cleeve was Commandant of the Shop for practically the whole of the war, from October 1914 to June 1918. His promotion in 1917 properly recognised his untiring efforts in a very responsible appointment. As Colonel Maurice-Jones writes:

HM King George V and Queen Mary with the Commandant and officers of the RMC after the presentation of Colours to the College in 1913.

Cleeve had marked the steady fall in the educational standard of cadets joining the Shop and was doing all he could to combat it. He appreciated that it was a problem of vital importance and took it up with the War Office and the head-masters of schools. His aim was to ensure that every cadet entering the Shop should have a sound knowledge of those subjects on which his military and technical training was to be grafted. This was most difficult as the educational level of schools fell steadily as the war went on. Cleeve demanded that the standard of the entrance examination should not be lowered, and that the examination itself should be altered to fit in with his requirements. Before he left the Shop, he had the satisfaction of seeing most of his recommendations put into effect.

One of the results of the lengthening of the course was that each batch of artillery cadets did a week's firing practise at Larkhill, which at least ensured that they did not start their commissioned service without ever having seen a gun fired. In June 1918 the passing-out inspection was taken by the Duke of Cambridge, and the following month King George visited the Academy, taking the salute at a ceremonial parade and seeing every aspect of the training. After a visit to the Chapel he addressed the cadets

120

and presented the Sword of Honour to Senior Under Officer C.H.F.D'A. McCarthy. When the Armistice came in November the number of cadets commissioned from the Royal Military Academy since the outbreak of war stood at 1,629.

SANDHURST, A PEACEFUL YEAR

At Sandhurst the doubling of the cadet establishment had involved more than the building of accommodation blocks and extra classrooms. For nearly a century there had never been a proper hospital building and successive surgeons had been forced to make do with the house originally built for the Adjutant at the east end of the Old Buildings, supplemented by an isolation ward built in the woods near the rifle ranges. Now a new hospital, specially designed and equipped, was built on the hill behind the new blocks, and in December 1913 the old hospital was taken over as the College headquarters. A considerably larger and more modern gymnasium was also required urgently, but unfortunately it was not ready for use until early in 1915.

During the summer term of 1914 there were two notable innovations, the first being a boxing tournament, marking the revival of the sport after a gap of thirteen years. The Commandant, having presented the prizes, 'hoped the meeting would be an annual event, even if it did not take place each term'. Equally noteworthy was the institution of a rifle and revolver meeting, which was held on the ranges at the back of the College and attracted nearly 500 entries. There were ten rifle events, the most important being an inter-company falling-plate shoot for teams of six, which was won by 'K' Company. There were five revolver competitions and a running-deer shoot in one of the miniature ranges.

All this took place in June, as did the last two fixtures against the Shop, both held at Woolwich. Sandhurst won the two-day cricket match by five wickets and the revolver match held the same weekend. The RMC inter-company cricket competition had already been decided, with 'H' Company gaining the Cup. Full details were given in the fourth annual issue of *The RMC Record*, and the article concluded with an appeal to 'the financial authorities', urging an immediate extension of the ground available for company and inter-company games. It was to be some years before this particular prayer was answered, although efforts were being made in other directions. Through the initiative of one of the company commanders the Oak Grove had been turned into a first-class polo ground, where some twenty-eight gentlemen cadets were able to play one day a week, and the Commandant had given permission for a pack of beagles to be started in the winter term.

121

On Monday 22 June His Majesty's birthday was celebrated. The Battalion paraded with all officers present at 7.15 a.m., and the rest of the day was observed as a holiday. The march-past was witnessed by a contingent from the Oxford University OTC which included Corporal HRH The Prince of Wales and which on the previous day had taken part in the church parade and attended the morning service in the Chapel. And so the last few weeks of term slipped by. The summer ball was held as usual in the gymnasium, with a dance floor in a large marquee on the edge of the cricket ground. Then came the end-of-term examinations and the half-yearly inspection, taken on this occasion by the Chief of the Imperial General Staff. The Commandant's report mentioned that the change-over to the eighteen-month course was now complete. There had been a marked improvement in shooting, and also in the standard of essays set in connection with the third-term English prize that had recently been instituted. For the third time running 'G' Company had gained the honourable distinction of being Champion Company at Arms. Sir Charles Douglas, in addressing the cadets, was in serious mood. He spoke at length on the subject of discipline, and reminded those passing out 'that what appealed to the British soldier more than anything else was a high sense of honour, justice and fairness on the part of his officers'. Nineteen days later mobilisation was ordered.

MOBILISATION AND BILLETS

The new senior term were commissioned immediately on mobilisation. Of the remainder, all who had done six months' training were put on a refresher course in tactics for four weeks and then commissioned. The newly arrived juniors went straight on to the emergency short course of three months' purely military training, and a tenth company was formed. As for the future, the entry age and abolition of fees were the same as at Woolwich, and the Civil Service Commissioners announced that there would be 350 cadetships to Sandhurst offered at the next entrance examination in a few weeks' time. As a footnote to the instructions the Commandant received shortly after mobilisation, there was a request to nominate eight to ten gentlemen cadets as observers with the Royal Flying Corps accompanying the Expeditionary Force. Some officers on the staff had disappeared to other appointments overnight, and to help a critical shortage the Commandant offered to reduce the establishment of officers to three per company, thereby releasing a further thirteen officers for active service abroad.

In November instructions came from the Military Secretary to raise the numbers under training to 960, a figure that was to include batches of temporary commissioned officers who would be put through a one-month course at the RMC. These officers were to be accommodated at the Staff College, which had closed at the beginning of the war. Between December 1914 and April 1916 no less than fifteen courses were run for the officers of the New Armies 'billeted out' at the Staff College. Then two extra companies of gentlemen cadets occupied the Staff College for a further sixteen months until the staff courses were restarted in September 1917.

THE RMC 1914–1918

Throughout the war the RMC continued to train cadets for regular commissions, and for the first year a three-month course remained in operation. By the end of 1915 the course had been extended whenever possible to six months, and the following year its length increased to eight months. Then throughout 1917 the training was based on a ten months' course, and finally in February 1918 a twelve-month course was introduced, together with the normal three terms. During the early years, however, the length of any one course was in reality tied to the constantly changing war situation and the often sudden and urgent need to find more and more officers, not only for the Western Front with its appalling casualties, but for the growing number of overseas theatres of war. In this connection there was also the growing commitment of the Indian Army. One officer who as a schoolboy had sat the RMC entrance examination at Burlington House in February 1915, hoping to get an Indian Army place, recalls:

When the result reached me early in April, a day after I left school, I read that an overflow from Sandhurst would be sent out to Quetta to the Staff College which had been closed at the outbreak of war. I accepted Quetta and sailed P. & O. on 17 April with fifty cadets, another fifty going by Anchor Line. There was a similar cadet college at Wellington Barracks in southern India, and the six-month courses, later extended, continued throughout the war. I should add that the Indian Army continued to receive a quota of young officers from Sandhurst as well.

At Sandhurst some of the most critical periods came in the first two years of the war. The Commandant from November 1914 to August 1916 was Brigadier General S.P. Rolt, CB, and he and his staff faced enormous problems running short courses, not only for the cadets, but also for young officers and company commanders of the New Armies. The demand for officers allowed no let-up, no breaks between courses, no leave. Instructors were constantly changing, as wounded officers took their turn until they were fit enough to be posted overseas again.

On 29 June 1916, two days before the Allied offensive on the Somme, the King and Queen paid a short visit to Sandhurst. They were in residence at

Royal Lodge, Aldershot, and drove over to spend the morning at the RMC. After a short parade Their Majesties made a tour of the College, visiting the riding school and the gymnasium and inspecting the outdoor work. The informality of the occasion and the interest shown in all the training was highlighted by Their Majesties returning two days later to be present at the church parade and attend divine service – the first occasion on which any sovereign had been present at a service in the Chapel.

In August, Brigadier General Stopford, who had commanded IX Corps at the Suvla Bay landing in Gallipoli, came back to Sandhurst and once again took over as Commandant. Many changes had taken place and more were to follow. In March 1916 the specialised cavalry company ('K' Company) had been abolished. All the Sandhurst cadets now went through the same short riding course, and in July 1916 we find the three senior companies being examined in riding and taking part in the Saddle and inter-company jumping competitions. During the period of the short courses there had been no time for special competitions or for playing the usual organised games, except on a completely *ad hoc* basis. The drill competition and the cross-country event in the Champion Company Competition were reintroduced, however, at the end of 1915, followed by the shooting and PT events. Also, with the start of the eight-month course, prizes were awarded for all the main military subjects, as well as for French and German, and athletic sports were held in the summer of 1916.

In the autumn of 1916, when the accommodation at the Staff College became available, the cadet establishment for the RMC was raised to 960. The actual strength in October was 695, somewhat down on the previous establishment of 780, but with lengthening courses and a steady intake of juniors the numbers quickly built up. A cadet who joined towards the end of 1916 describes conditions:

The course at this time was ten months, but later extended to twelve. The Staff College, which had been accommodating some OTC men, was cleared, and two new companies, 'M' and 'O', were formed with gentlemen cadets from the Old and New Buildings. I was first posted to 'G' Company on the first floor of the Old Building, where each cadet had his own room, but on transferring to the Staff College, with large rooms, four or five shared a room. The training was quite severe, with cross-country runs in a certain time and trench-digging. The full musketry course was fired on Bisley ranges; the transport there, and indeed everywhere, was on cycles.

During 1917 all the remaining Champion Company competitions were reintroduced, and an interesting innovation was an inter-company map

Newly joined 'juniors' at the Royal Military College in 1917.

and compass race, for which Colonel Paly gave a cup. More time was also allocated for playing the conventional sports. The number of tennis courts had already been doubled to over forty during the earlier period of the war as an emergency measure; now the limiting factor was more the shortage of pitches. Here a start was made through the arrival of a detachment of the Canadian Forestry Corps. Their first task was to clear a site for the new isolation hospital being built on Windsor Ride, but they soon turned their attention to the area in front of the New Buildings. The fringe of firs and scrub between the pavilion and the Wish Stream was cleared, and the road that circled the running track was moved to the edge of the stream. This work completely opened up the view from the 'Sappers' bridge towards the New Buildings, and in due course, after the ground had been properly drained, provided a major extension to the playing fields. This indeed was forecast in an article in *The RMC Record*, which also mentioned future plans for a fine new canteen and a swimming bath.

The same issue of the journal printed an appeal for funds to enlarge the Chapel as a memorial to former gentlemen cadets who had lost their lives during the war. The appeal was signed by Major General Stopford, two former Commandants (Rolt and Capper), the Assistant Commandant Colonel Paly and the Chaplain and his predecessor, the Reverend Harry Blackburne. Beneath the signatures was printed the following:

Three Years of the Great War 4 August 1914–4 August 1917
Died for King, Country and Freedom   2,357

There then followed details of honours and awards over the same period: 21 VCs, 734 DSOs and 804 MCs, together with over 500 honours and 600 foreign decorations.

A cadet who joined in January 1918 gives his impression of what it was like to do a one-year course in ten months:

We were drilled and drilled and had lots of riding, gym and rifle instruction, together with elementary tactics, but I don't remember doing much digging. We were taught law up to courts martial and administration up to battalion level. We started at 6 a.m. and worked all day, and with lectures after mess, this took us up to 11 p.m. The atmosphere was that life was going to be short. I well remember cycling to London and back on many occasions, as we were not allowed on trains without permission.

This was a year that brought a series of royal occasions, vividly remembered by some who were cadets at the time. In the middle of June a two-day athletics meeting was held on the new cricket field (the present 1st XI ground). On the afternoon of the second day Their Majesties, accompanied by the Princess Mary, arrived in time to take tea and see the final events for the Inter-Company Challenge Shield, the one-mile relay and the obstacle race. Queen Mary graciously presented the prizes, and a special presentation was made to 'Jack' Clarke, the well-known groundsman of the College, who had completed thirty-three years' devoted service and whose untiring efforts had kept the grounds in perfect condition throughout the war years. The following day the royal party returned to attend the church parade and service.

By the beginning of the winter term of 1918 the accommodation at the Staff College had been handed back and the course extended to the pre-war eighteen months. The Allied offensives in Palestine and Salonika were about to be launched, and on the Western Front, after five months' bitter fighting, the Germans had been halted and the Allied assault on the Hindenburg line had begun. At last a light was shining at the end of the tunnel. In November a very special honour was bestowed on the Royal Military College. Some time earlier King George had decided to present a Banner to be carried on parade by the Champion Company, in this way associating himself with what he regarded as 'an excellent [competition] for promoting efficiency and *esprit de corps*'. The ceremony was to take place in the forecourt of Buckingham Palace on 7 November, a date which turned out to be four days before the Armistice was announced.

At Sandhurst, as a member of the Guard of Honour well recalls, the preparations had started almost on the first day of term. Under the eye of the Adjutant, Major Dalrymple-Hamilton, the whole Battalion had been marched round and round the Square until, by a stern process of elimination, there were remaining four under officers, four cadet sergeants and 100 gentlemen cadets. This total in fact included some twenty-five cadet NCOs who were to be temporarily 'stripped' to serve in the ranks. Then day after day there was drill and more drill, until every movement had been rehearsed a hundred times over.

Accompanying the Guard of Honour on the train up to Waterloo were a number of supernumeraries to act as batmen to see that not a single speck of dust or any blemish spoilt the combined effect of brushing, pressing, burnishing and polishing of uniform, arms and equipment. Tradition has it that the responsibility for carrying the Adjutant's best tunic on the journey to London fell to Gentlemen Cadet Prince Henry, later HRH The Duke of Gloucester and a Field Marshal. Special permission had been given for the cadets to march from the station to the Palace with fixed bayonets, and they were accompanied by two Guards' bands.

In the forecourt of the Palace a distinguished gathering was assembled, which included the Chief of the Imperial General Staff and most of the Army Council. Amongst the specially invited guests were parents of the cadets who were on parade. Before handing over the Banner, the King expressed his hope that 'it will be looked upon as an emblem of honour, and that the contests for its possession will help to foster those chivalrous and sporting instincts so characteristic of the British race'. Under Officer the Earl of Brecknock of the Champion Company ('A' Company) then replied, ending: 'We are very justly proud of the interest Your Majesty is graciously pleased to take in the Royal Military College, of which we are all determined to do our best to prove ourselves in some degree worthy.' The ceremonial that followed the presentation included the trooping of the 'King George V Banner', and as *The Times* commented, 'the cadets carried out their evolutions with remarkable precision, and their performance would have done credit to a highly trained company of Guardsmen'.

The following summer the ceremony of handing over the Banner to a new Champion Company took place as part of the end-of-term passing-out parade. The procedure was identical to that followed in the present Sovereign's Parade, except that the Banner was not trooped. The following day Major General Stopford was due to hand over command, and in his last end-of-term report he included a backward glance over the war years. Between the outbreak of war and the middle of November 1918 thirty-five cadets had been awarded the VC and 5,131 had been commissioned from the College. The Roll of Honour contained the names of 3,274 former cadets, and an appeal had been launched for funds to enlarge the Chapel as their memorial.

THE REBUILDING OF THE CHAPEL

The rebuilding of the Chapel will always be associated with three men: Major General Stopford who conceived the idea, A.C. Martin who drew up the plans, and Padre Blackburne, the Chaplain who returned to Sandhurst at the end of the war. The fact that the seating capacity of Christ Church was quite inadequate had been recognised for some years, but how to extend the building had never been decided, and with the outbreak of war the whole question was in abeyance. When Stopford returned to Sandhurst he was again faced with the problem. He saw not merely a shortage of accommodation which needed remedying but equally an opportunity to build a national memorial to the former cadets who had given their lives in the Great War.

On the staff at the time was Captain A.C. Martin, RE, who was also a Fellow of the Royal Institute of British Architects. He suggested that the Chapel could be enlarged by striking across the original building with a new east and west end and considerably increasing the size of the nave. From this simple idea developed the plans exhibited at the Royal Academy which later resulted in the beautiful Chapel of today. Credit must be shared between Captain Martin, who was appointed architect for the whole scheme, and Major General Stopford, who devoted himself to its direction.

The Chaplain in the immediate post-war years was Harry Blackburne, and to him fell the responsibility for carrying on this dedicated task of overseeing the incorporation of regimental and individual memorials and indeed raising the necessary funds, for the question of cost had become a very serious consideration. Whereas money for an extension had been available before the war, this was no longer the case. Now the very bricks for the walls had to be paid for by private subscription, and in the lean years that followed the end of the war the raising of funds became increasingly difficult. In the end the building of the new west end had to be delayed for lack of funds for many years, and the original plans for a great central tower had to be abandoned.

The new east end was finished early in 1921 and that part of the Chapel was dedicated on 5 May by the Archbishop of Canterbury. Again there was an interval of a year while great efforts were made to raise further funds; then work was started on incorporating the original structure into the new nave. A number of regimental memorial tablets were placed in this part of the enlarged Chapel, and these were dedicated on 5 November 1922 by the Bishop of Oxford. In the lean years that followed great efforts were made to raise the funds to complete the west end. Finally, Lord Halifax, Lord Privy Seal and a former Secretary of State for War, arranged a public grant towards the cost of the fabric, and the remaining memorial tablets were installed.

During the whole of this period King George V had shown the greatest interest in the Chapel, attending the Sunday church parade on several occasions. His gift of a bible on St George's Day 1923 was an expression of his affection for the Chapel and what it stands for. The door at the west end is Sandhurst's memorial to the Sovereign to whom the Chapel owes so much. The west end was completed early in 1937, and this final portion of the Chapel was dedicated on 2 May by the Archbishop of Canterbury in the presence of TRH The Duke and Duchess of Gloucester, HRH The Princess Royal, The Earl of Harewood, Major General the Earl of Athlone and representatives of every regiment of the Army.

CHAPTER 10

Peacetime Solutions

POST-WAR SANDHURST

In the Great War Britain lost a complete generation, and the cost in material and wealth had been enormous. In the aftermath came changes, little recognised in their beginnings, but inevitable and pervasive. Not only was the structure of society changing, but by the 1930s the country faced the crippling realities of a worldwide trade depression. The return to peace conditions brought the inevitable cutbacks in manpower and finance for the Armed Services.

In the early days after the war the cadet colleges were busy 'getting back to normal'. Their role was unaltered; their establishments were much the same as at the outbreak of hostilities, but the pressure was off. In 1919 Sandhurst for the first time entered an eight for Henley. This was the first post-war Henley Regatta, and the RMC found that the only event they could row in was the Open Eights. They were drawn against Cambridge University II (who went on to win the event) and lost by three-quarters of a length after a very close race.

Another highlight of the same summer was a tank field day which was held on Barossa, the training area behind the College. This was the first time any cadets had seen a demonstration of the capabilities of the tank, let alone taken part in a joint exercise. The demonstration had been arranged for the students of the Staff College. Four Medium 'C' Light Tanks (25 tons, 15 m.p.h. max.) were put through their paces, supported by two Bristol Fighters in a simple attack scheme, with the cadet battalion providing the infantry. Bandsmen, suitably hidden, set off charges to simulate a barrage, to the complete mystification of the local populace, who had turned out in their hundreds to see how battles were won.

With the start of the two-year course in 1920, a complete reorganisation took place. The ten companies were amalgamated to make five large companies, each of four platoons, and the Senior Division provided the under officers and cadet NCOs throughout. For each company there was a company commander, seven other officers and two attached French officers, plus two staff sergeants and four sergeants. On the Headquarter's staff there was a gunner, a sapper and a PT officer.

With more married officers than before the war, the problem of insufficient quarters eventually arose. To add point to the situation, the Surgeon had his own quarters condemned as unfit for human habitation and had to be moved into the Square while a wooden bungalow was built on Windsor Ride. In the meantime married quarters were required for the Adjutant, so it was decided that the Surgeon's old quarters must be completely renovated. These were eventually handed over to the Adjutant and renamed Lake House. Within a few years a little colony of wooden bungalows was established amongst the trees just off Windsor Ride. Each consisted of two huts joined side to side and for over half a century provided a home for successive generations of officers, and latterly professors and lecturers also, before they in turn were declared 'unfit for human habitation'. This time, however, there was no reprieve!

In December 1920 the end-of-term examinations included two new papers, on military history and the history and geography of the British Empire, and within a year a number of officers of the Army Education Corps had joined the staff in support of an expanding syllabus of general education. The old Chapel behind the Grand Entrance was set up as an educational library, with £250 for books added to the following year's estimates. The College was quietly settling down to a pattern of life that contrasted sharply with the hectic war years. Up till now it had been possible to plan changes; soon they would be dictated by a deteriorating economic climate. Throughout the war the dress for mess had been a dinner jacket, now it was to be blue patrol. Games were once more in the ascendancy, but emphasis was placed on those connected with the Assault at Arms. Inter-company leagues in the major sports no longer counted towards the Champion Company Competition, but competitions in bayonet, sabre, foil, boxing and PT all carried marks. To these were added the marks for riding, weapon training, drill, and for the first time the 'work' of each term.

The sports teams were now able to travel to away fixtures in one of the RMC motor lorries, named 'Dorcas' and 'Squirrel'. They were fitted with wooden benches and had been purchased from College funds. The new Commandant, Major General Sir R.B. Stephens, KCB, CMG, was allocated a staff car, one of a pool of three kept at the Staff College. In the shadow of this 'mechanisation', however, the horse remained in as strong a position as ever. All the company commanders had chargers, and every cadet was put through a thorough and well-organised course in equitation. When the gross cost per cadet rose between 1921 and 1922 by over £100 to

£373. 14s. 3d. per annum, one of the reasons given was the increased cost of maintaining the proper number of horses for the College. It was at this time that orders went out that cadets should be 'encouraged' to visit the stables after church on Sunday, 'to see what could be done in the way of dressing stables with materials officially available for the purpose'.

Not only was the cost of fodder going up, so was the cost of living. The size of entries had begun to drop, and there had been a number of 'with-drawals', as the inevitable result of the ending of the war and the reintroduction of fees. In 1920 fourteen scholarships valued at £40 were made available each half-year to gentlemen cadets who had successfully completed their first year of the course and whose fathers had been commissioned through the wartime officer cadet battalions. Soon afterwards all gentlemen cadets on commissioning were given a grant towards their uniform of £50, or £150 where full dress was required for the Household Cavalry or the Guards. To raise money to continue the rebuilding of the Chapel a two-day gala and fête was held in May 1921. The attendance of the Prince of Wales drew big crowds, and nearly £6,000 was raised.

In the following year, 1922, it was decided that the fees at Woolwich and Sandhurst must be raised. King's Cadets were still admitted free, but otherwise the annual rate went up to £200 for the sons of private gentlemen, while the fees for sons of serving officers varied from £105 to £55 according to the father's rank. The lowest rate also applied to the sons of deceased officers and other ranks, except where the family had been left 'in pecuniary need', when only £20 was asked. At the same time a comparison of those commissioned in 1922 with those of 1913 showed that the numbers

Bridge-building instruction at the RMA Woolwich in 1919.

and types of candidates were also changing. While the output from Woolwich of around 130 had been maintained by the injection of a dozen or so King's Cadets and other nominations, the figures for Sandhurst showed a serious falling off from 337 to 234 in the numbers qualifying for entry through the competitive examination. Furthermore, in spite of an increase in the number of King's Cadetships from 27 to 46 and Head-master's nominations, from 7 to 39, the total number of cadets commissioned from the RMC had dropped from 371 to 329. There had also been a fall in the numbers commissioned from the universities from 74 to 17, and direct commissioning from the Reserve Forces had been abolished. Compared with 1913, the total number of commissions granted in the Army in 1922 showed a drop of 200, a situation that was causing grave concern.

VISCOUNT HALDANE'S COMMITTEE

The result was that a parliamentary committee was appointed under the chairmanship of Viscount Haldane to examine the whole question of officer entry for the Army. The subsequent report published in June 1923 is noteworthy for its incisive approach. Dealing first with the supply of cadets, the Committee felt that the shortage:

... was in part at least due to the belief of the public that the profession of officer in the Army was not one which called for as high qualities as that to be found in the analogous profession of the Navy or in many other professions. The some-what paradoxical inference presented itself that in order to increase competition for entry ... it had become necessary to ask not less but more from the would-be entrant. In other words, we have to seek primarily an improved type of entrant and to provide adequate opportunities for this type, rather than reduce standards.

The Committee considered that too much emphasis had been given to some of the proposals of the Akers-Douglas Committee, and that attempts by the cadet colleges to turn out technically completely trained officers 'had resulted in the premature arrest of intellectual development and reduced the output of officers fit to rise to the highest positions in the Army'. The lower age for cadet entry should be eighteen, candidates should possess the Oxford and Cambridge Joint Board School Certificate, and the Civil Service Entrance Examination should be reconstituted. The courses at both Woolwich and Sandhurst should be eighteen months, after which gunner officers should complete their technical training at the School of Artillery, Larkhill, and sapper officers should do a combined course at the School of Military Engineering, Chatham, and Cambridge University.

FOUNDATION SUBJECTS

Much else emerged in the body of the report. For instance, at the RMA 'measures to inculcate discipline were considered unnecessarily intrusive'; the sleeping accommodation was inadequate, which 'militates considerably against individual study', for which more time was required, particularly for the mathematics and chemistry courses. The teaching of history and military history also needed more attention. Finally, assuming that the cadets went on to Larkhill and Chatham, the system of bifurcation should be abandoned.

Sandhurst presented a somewhat different problem. While on the average the intellectual level of the cadets might be lower than at Woolwich, there would be a wider bracket of abilities. Much of the present technical or semi-technical teaching should be retained, but in spite of a shortened course it was clearly desirable that time should be devoted to general education, 'firstly, to develop respect for and interest in intellectual study for its own sake, not for any immediate reward; and secondly, to cultivate independence of mental activity, the habit of using books, of thinking, speaking and writing about some worthy object'. Cadets must be trained to read for themselves, to study from a number of sources and search out information, to weigh opinions and compare different points of view. To this end the single subject most likely to provide a 'foundational' basis for the Army officer was the study of history, and in particular military history. As for languages, these should be studied at more advanced levels. The question of amalgamation of the two colleges was dismissed on financial grounds, and the Committee went so far as to express their opinion that, whatever the advantages otherwise might be, 'real amalgamation is impossible, as two different standards and very different courses are required'.

The broad recommendations of the report were implemented almost immediately, and so the pattern for cadet education for the next decade and a half came into being. Once the curricula had been adjusted there were relatively few changes before 1939, and those that took place reflected the attempts, often frustrated by financial stringency, to prepare for such changes as mechanisation, and to broaden the pattern of general education.

CAR MASTERSHIP

At Woolwich classroom instruction on the internal combustion engine had started in 1920, and driving instruction was introduced the following year, a single three-ton lorry being all that was available. While 1927 was the year that the decision was made by the General Staff that the Army should be reorganised for armoured and mechanised warfare, 1928 was the year

The Royal Memorial Chapel, Sandhurst. The Chapel was enlarged between 1919 and 1937. This view shows the nave and the east end in 1979.

The Indian Army Memorial Room. Situated behind the Grand Entrance in the Old Buildings, this was the Chapel from 1813 to 1870.

East Building, completed in 1970 and now named Victory College. In the foreground is the Prince Imperial Statue brought from Woolwich.

when there was a further swing away from technical training at the Shop in preference for a more general and scientific education. Driving instruction and gas training were both set aside completely. Moreover, the privilege of using a private car or motorcycle on leave was withdrawn after two serious accidents in which civilians were involved.

The ban remained until the end of 1936, at which time the Chief of the Imperial General Staff was urging that 'increased instruction in mechanically propelled vehicles, especially driving' should be given. In fact 'car mastership' had been taught since 1931 by a team of Royal Engineer officers specially posted to the RMA, but although given the more grandiose title of 'Car Course – IC and Heavy Oil Engine', the instruction dealt solely with the theory of engines and practical maintenance and repairs, and no cadets were being taught to drive. The Commandant unsuccessfully tried to pass this responsibility on to Larkhill. The ball was then passed to the Military College of Science, who could only spare two vehicles, which were patently insufficient to compete with the number of young officers involved. So eighteen months later, after a heated battle with the Treasury, the War Office gave the Commandant of the RMA seven instructors, two 30-cwt lorries and five 15-cwt trucks and told him to get on with teaching all cadets to drive.

AN EXPANDING SYLLABUS

In some contrast to this situation instruction in riding and horse mastership retained a consistently high place in the batting order throughout the whole of the inter-war period. When the eighteen-month course was introduced in 1924, a total of 178 hours were allocated. By 1930 the plea was for more general education, and riding had dropped to 144 hours. It was, however, running second to the top scorer, strategy and tactics, which had 150 hours, and well ahead of mathematics and science, both with 129, and drill with 120 hours. At this date the internal combustion engine scored under 10. Military history, with 38 hours, was part of the tactics and strategy course. General Education, taught by civilian professors and lecturers, covered British constitutional history, geography, economics, and imperial and foreign affairs, which together were given 111 hours. The cadet was also required to opt for two of the following 'alternative' subjects: French, German, mechanical and engineering science, advanced mathematics, chemistry applied to warfare, and electricity and wireless, each being allocated 66 hours spread over the last two terms. Taking the two key subjects of mathematics and science and the other educational subjects together, these took up 36 per cent of the available periods, and the marks allocated were 45 per cent of the total over the

Mission Française, Sandhurst, 1919–20.

whole course. Current affairs lectures were held in the evenings and some periods were set aside for private study.

At Sandhurst in the early 1920s there were ten French officers attached to teach their language. When the Haldane Report was published there were still seven at the RMC and four at the RMA, and this must have encouraged the Committee to propose a higher entry standard so as to make better use of this expert instruction. Sadly the financiers thought otherwise, and in 1926 the establishments were cut and the number of French officers was reduced to one at each college.

The post-war two-year course had also included a study of the history and geography of the Empire and imperial organisation. The juniors were expected to read up the background, and in the second year there were a number of special lectures. During 1921, however, twelve Army Education Corps officers arrived to teach the 'educational' subjects. By the 1930s this educational element had expanded until it occupied about a third of the available time, the subjects being: Britain and the Commonwealth, imperial military geography, modern history, leading to lectures on current affairs, and economics. In addition every cadet had to opt for one 'voluntary' subject, having a choice of French, German, economics, mechanical engineering, or electricity and wireless. These educational subjects together carried about 40 per cent of the available marks.

A further innovation was the arrival of selected NCOs in September 1922 to take the second year of the Sandhurst course with a view to commissioning. The first batch numbered thirty-two, and each cadet had to be under twenty-four and unmarried. Being on a year's course, they were known as 'Y' cadets. The scheme proved most valuable, and when the eighteen-month course came in, their successors, who had to be a year younger, did the full time. It was not until 1928 that Woolwich took the first Army cadet, as they were then called. He was Arthur Hill, Probationer Artificer RA, who was commissioned into the Royal Signals, and from then on there were usually one or two in every year at the Shop.

Direct commissioning into the Royal Signals had started from Woolwich in 1924, and to compete with the expansion of the corps 125 young officers joined from the RMA over the next three years. But both Woolwich and Sandhurst were having increasing difficulties in attracting sufficient candidates. By the mid-1930s the RMA was down to 175 cadets, the lowest figure since 1908. The depression had affected the RMC rather earlier, with the numbers falling to 470 in February 1929. A year later the four companies could muster 529, and the junior batch was 190 strong, but unfortunately this improvement was barely maintained and at the end of 1937 the cadet strength was only around 550.

While the country struggled to recover from the years of acute financial depression every possible economy had to be made. By 1931 the cost to public funds of maintaining a cadet stood at £562 per annum, and both colleges had to find means of reducing their budgets. At Sandhurst, for instance, the cut was set at £20,000. The appointment of Assistant Commandant was abolished and the instructional establishment reduced by six officers, and by most of the Royal Engineers detachment and a number of the civilian employees, old soldiers who had given long and loyal service to the College. The makeweight at the end of the list of economies that was finally agreed on was a reduction in the rate for feeding the cadets.

In a rapidly deteriorating international situation a committee under the Marquess of Willingdon, struggling with the problem of what was now a grave shortage of officers, considered that the cadet colleges must remain the main source of supply, rather than extension of any system for promotion from the ranks. The fees, however, were too high 'in view of the general impoverishment of the classes from which officers have been or might have been drawn', and the War Office must go outside the public schools to get the necessary numbers – a point that Lord Haldane had made over ten years previously. The lowest rate of fees had already been reduced in cases of hardship. Now, under similar circumstances, officers' or servicemen's sons could be accepted at minimal fees or be given free places, as were the King's Cadets.

INDIAN AND OTHER OVERSEAS CADETS

These recurrent difficulties of recruiting officers for the British Army made no apparent difference to the high prestige of the cadet colleges in the eyes of countries abroad. Soon after the end of the First World War a scheme was launched for the gradual replacement of British officers in the Indian Army with Sandhurst-trained Indian officers, and the first two Indian cadets joined the RMC in 1919. Between then and 1934 well over 150 Indian cadets successfully completed the course and were commissioned into Indian infantry regiments. Indian cadets were subsequently commissioned from Dehra Dun into all branches of the Indian Army. Meanwhile Woolwich had stepped in to reinforce the success of the Indian cadets at Sandhurst by offering a limited number of vacancies over a five-year period. The first to apply were Aserappa and Gyani, and the former writes of his experiences:

At that time I was completing my education at a public school in London, but before being accepted I had to pass the week-long examination at Burlington Gardens, which included an interview, with sufficient marks to get my only choice – the RMA. During December 1929 I was informed that I had obtained sufficient marks and been selected for the RMA. Under normal circumstances I would have joined the following January, but as Gyani could not arrive in time from India I had to wait for his arrival so as not to gain a six months' seniority over him. Thus, on 29 September 1930, Gyani and I were the first two under the scheme to enter the RMA and start our training, which ended late in December 1931.

I passed out of the RMA with sufficient marks to obtain an Engineer commission on 28 January 1932, and after a further three-year period of training in No. 27 Young Officers' Batch REs at the School of Military Engineering and a degree course at Cambridge University, was posted to India during April 1935 to the Unattached List Indian Army, which was the normal practice at that time for all officers joining the Indian Army. As Gyani did not do so well academically at the RMA he was given a commission in the Gunners, and after completing his training at Larkhill was posted to the Indian Artillery.

Both these cadets rose to the rank of Major General, Gyani as the Director of Artillery at Army Headquarters, New Delhi, and Aserappa as the first Engineer-in-Chief to the Defence Ministry.

Of the twelve Indian cadets who passed through the Shop in the next few years, eight were commissioned into the Indian Sappers and Miners and the remainder into the Indian Artillery or the Corps of Signals. The scheme was an undoubted success and, apart from their distinguished war service, many former Indian cadets from Woolwich and Sandhurst filled posts of the highest responsibility after Independence.

Between the wars 254 cadets from overseas entered Sandhurst and 70 entered Woolwich. Apart from those from India, a significant number passed into Sandhurst from other Commonwealth countries. These were mostly from New Zealand, cadets who afterwards joined the British Army or returned to their own country, or from South Africa, most of whose cadets were destined for the Indian Army. Otherwise both at Woolwich and Sandhurst the pattern was much the same, with a sprinkling at any one time of cadets from Egypt, Iraq, Siam, China and Persia. At Sandhurst the largest contingent turned out to be the Chinese, and in the early 1930s the first batch of 'Honorary Chinese Cadets' caused quite a stir. They were given several months to acclimatise themselves and learn essential British ways as well as the language. The Chinese squad playing football by numbers on the pitch opposite the New Buildings' classrooms brought many a lecture to a hilarious halt, as did their efforts to perform the customary 'cavalry drill' on bicycles, a feat often complicated by the bicycles having had their brakes loosened by persons unknown shortly beforehand. Their enthusiasm was unlimited, and bicycle drill was assiduously practised at the weekends with many dramatic pile-ups on the gravel tracks leading down from Barossa.

THE 'TROOP'

Throughout the 1930s riding continued to be the most popular part of the course at Woolwich. On lunch parade, before the cadets marched off, the order was given, 'Fall out anyone wanting to buy a horse.' This was the opportunity to put one's name down for a voluntary ride the same afternoon. The charge was nominal – the extra duty pay of the trooper who turned out the horse down at the barracks. Cadets in the top rides were occasionally taken out for a day's hunting by officers on the staff.

One of the riding instructors was John Lynch who, after having instructed at the Army School of Equitation and at Sandhurst, returned to the Riding Establishment Royal Horse Artillery for the last ten years before it closed on mobilisation.

My grandfather, father and myself were riding instructors at 'The Troop', responsible for riding instruction and sword drill at the Shop. . . . some of the great horsemen in the RHA were on courses under my father in the early 1900s. In fact Lieutenant Colonel Lucas was the first Chief Instructor when Weedon

141

was formed, and other well-known instructors from the Shop were: Dolly deFonblanque, Buggins Brunker, Ted Howard Vyse, Jock Campbell, VC, Charles Allfrey of 8th Army fame, and Keith Dunn.

Amongst the cadets I myself instructed there was Orde Wingate, a very lone and reserved type, and King Farouk, who was very charming and very lazy but did exactly what he was told. The King of Siam we reckoned was the best vaulter we ever had. Possibly the nicest horseman among them was the Maharajah of Jaipur, who offered me Master of Horse to Jaipur at the end of his year at the RMA. He later came over to England with the Jaipur Polo Team, which consisted of four Jaipur princes who were during their stay unbeatable. Every time I am at home and go to Woolwich and pass the Royal Military Academy I think of the great people that have passed in and out of its gates. With the deflation of everything military in England, it seems more like a dream than reality.

SOME REMINISCENCES

A cadet at the Shop from September 1930 to December 1931 recalls:

George Baker, later Field Marshal Sir Geoffrey Baker, was SUO of our term. Aserappa and Gyani, the first two Indian cadets, joined at the same time. On the staff we had Captain, later General, Sir Cameron Nicholson, and Captain, later Lieutenant General, Sir Ian Jacob. Towards the end of my first term practically all the cadet sergeants and corporals lost their stripes as a result of riotous behaviour returning from the last Shop-Sandhurst rugger match ever to be played at Richmond. Subsequently the rank of cadet sergeant was abolished and the corporals no longer wore stripes but had a badge of rank on their shoulder straps. In the summer of 1931, due to the financial crisis, we travelled to Aldershot on bicycles, organised as cavalry. The journey took us two days!

There was nothing new about the cadets 'marching' to and from camp, and the column staged at Hounslow Barracks to avoid the daytime traffic.

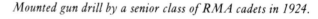

Mounted gun drill by a senior class of RMA cadets in 1924.

A cadet of the 1927–28 period found the RMC very horse-orientated:

As regards the 'Internal Combustion Engine', I am certain we had no instruction, or if we did, it was so little that it made no impression. We were divided into eight rides; No. 1 was almost entirely cavalry candidates, No. 2 was those who had done some hunting, and so on, down to those who had never ridden. I was put into No. 2 as I had hunted, and I managed to stay there. Hunting leave was given one day a week, but no chargers were available, so it was only those with their own horses; or one could hire locally – which I did. The Garth included a race for GCs in their point-to-point. It was quite alarming as there were generally some twenty runners, which made for congestion at the first jump. The race was run in uniform, but with point-to-point caps with khaki cloth covers.

In my brother's time (1922–24) after the passing-out parade the senior term used to take the Napoleonic guns from the front of the Old Building and put them in the lake. This practice ceased just before my time, when the Commandant kept the senior term back a day to pull them out again.

Boy Browning, afterwards a Lieutenant General, was the most efficient of Adjutants. Sergeant Major Brittain was the drill sergeant of my company – No. 4. On one memorable battalion parade, after rehearsing the march-past several times, Boy ordered the drill sergeants not to give the step, but from the rear of No. 4 came Brittain's stentorian 'Left-Right-LEFT'. Then, to the joy of 4 Company, the Adjutant said, 'Sergeant Major Brittain, get off parade.'

Some GCs found signing in after weekend leave rather an ordeal. The orderly officer sat at a table at the entrance of the Old Building. Many would not have passed a breathalyser test, but as long as some sort of signature was attempted and the GC remained upright most orderly officers were satisfied; if not, a charge of drunkenness was treated very seriously by the Commandant!

The maintenance of discipline and gentlemanly behaviour had its lighter moments, as another former cadet recalls:

In the summer of 1932 a certain GC 'liberated' a tankard from the bar of the Queen's Hotel, Farnborough, where a famous barmaid called Kitty, a very presentable type, presided. She obviously knew the tankard had been nicked by a GC, so the RMC was informed. It was just after the last parade one morning when the CSM of 5 Company, 'Windy' Hughes of the Coldstream Guards, ordered the Company to parade outside the Company steps wearing civilian clothes on their top halves, but in order to save time, retaining whatever they were wearing on the lower half. It was a strange spectacle. Our lower halves presented a medley of plus-fours and puttees for those who had been drilling, breeches and leggings for the equitators, and white flannels for those just back from PT. One GC aroused the wrath of the CSM by turning out wearing a clergyman's top half! Looking across to the other end of the Old Building Square we could see that a similar performance was taking place outside 4 Company.

In due course we saw a small party bearing down on the Company, consisting of Captain Norman Gwatkin, the Adjutant, a most imposing figure, over six foot, with a large ginger moustache and the most highly polished field boots I've ever seen. With him was Battalion Sergeant Major Dobson, Grenadier Guards, and, lo and behold, Kitty from the Queen's Hotel. This small party walked down the ranks, with Kitty, like an inspecting general, scrutinising each cadet. It transpired that she had inspected all four RMC companies in turn. Sandhurst has been inspected by royalty, and by many famous field marshals and generals, but surely never before or since by a barmaid! In fact the culprit was a member of 5 Company, but perhaps Kitty did not recognise him or was not prepared to pick him out. Not long after, the same cadet put up another 'black' and was removed from the RMC.

INSTRUCTORS LOOK BACK

Some of the teaching at this period would seem to have been handled on a rather loose rein. One officer who was told in the autumn of 1931 that he was to go to Sandhurst as a company commander early the following year describes his experiences on paying a preliminary visit:

I discovered that I would also be expected to teach 'The History of the British Army', one of the subjects in the newly introduced syllabus, to the whole of the junior division. With no qualifications at all for tackling the subject, I had to spend much of my spare time, while still on the staff of a London TA Division, in the library of the Royal United Services Institute. Even so, during my first term I lived a very hand-to-mouth existence from the teaching point of view, only just managing to keep abreast with my lectures. It was not of great help that I was never given any sort of syllabus of my subject, nor, as a guide, any programmes or precis used by my predecessor. I was left entirely to my own devices. All I remember being told was that the three hours weekly allotted to my subject should be divided into a lecture, private study and a tutorial. I had not the remotest idea of what was meant by the last named, and had to make enquiries! I had to deal with the juniors of all four companies, so every week I had to repeat the same lecture, direct the same private study and tutorial four times. Not an easy thing to do with the same degree of enthusiasm each time.

The other company commanders taught tactics or administration to the seniors, but as I only dealt in the 'hall of study' with juniors, I found it most difficult to perform what I regarded as the most important of a company commander's tasks – to get to know the cadets under his command, particularly in their last term before passing out for commissioning. In my opinion the idea of widening the Sandhurst syllabus to include non-military or semi-military subjects was theoretically right.

Another officer who rose to high rank recalls:

I was a cadet in the early 1920s. Most cadets stayed as GCs throughout the two-years course and in the same platoon, and we got used to our responsibilities through the normal command structure and the promotion system. Looking back, there was not enough on man-management, which is so tied in with morale. In military history the lessons were not brought out, and in the study of tactics there was no attempt to think about co-operation with armour.

In 1937 I went back as a company instructor, the qualification for which was to have been adjutant in one's own unit. These were the happiest years of my life, with wonderful opportunities for both organising and playing games. But there was no camp at either period when I was at Sandhurst, and the only war-related practical work in 1939 was digging trenches against air attack.

A FAMILY SPIRIT

When Major General Goschen took over as Commandant of the Shop in 1934 several of the sporting fixtures with Sandhurst and Cranwell were abandoned, leaving only athletics, cricket, Rugby, soccer, hockey, fencing, boxing, and golf (Sandhurst only), with the annual riding competition with Sandhurst continuing under the guise of training. While some gladiatorial

Joint parade and service for British Legion contingents and RMC cadets on the First XI cricket ground at Sandhurst in 1931.

contests no longer featured in the calendar, games continued to play a major role in the life of the Academy, and while modern pentathlon was given up, the Sailing Club continued to grow. A cadet who joined in 1936 remembers how well the games were run by members of the staff:

Each one was a specialist in a particular sport. The rugger was run by Jack Hardy and Victor Pike, both internationals, and the cricket by Tiger Urquhart. We took the matches against Cranwell and Sandhurst very seriously. The teams in training sat at a separate table and were fed on steaks! Amongst the lecturers there was 'Tiny' Considine, a Cambridge rugger blue, and 'Steve' (J.W. Stevenson), who organised the golf. In fact everyone was involved in one way or another.

This pervading family spirit is underlined by an instructor who had been a cadet at Sandhurst and later transferred into the Royal Signals: 'The Shop was a much more intimate place and the staff were totally integrated. On Public Day all the officers and lecturers paraded together opposite the cadets, and between us we covered every game and activity.'

The families were not left out either. The young bride of a gunner officer recalls:

We were a very happy, close-knit family, and we all joined in with whatever was going on. Of course there were the big occasions, such as the Summer Ball before the passing-out, but I well remember cycling in from Blackheath, where we lived 'off strength' as my husband was under thirty, to watch the games. Then there were the church parades, with everyone there and their children, and the Chapel service with the cadet choir and Victor Pike's wonderful short sermons.

Soon the last fixtures against Sandhurst and Cranwell would be held, the playing fields would be deserted, and later the Chapel would become a garrison church. During the last winter term the Rugby team beat both Sandhurst and Cranwell without losing a point, results that were also matched by the soccer team. The following spring the Hockey XI drew against Sandhurst and beat Cranwell, while the boxing team beat the RAF College but lost to Sandhurst. Then came the Triangular Athletics Sports and the Fencing Match at Olympia, in both of which Cranwell took first place, with the Shop coming second in the athletics but third in the fencing. The cricket results were equally disappointing for the Shop, a seven-wickets defeat by the RMC and a draw with Cranwell. So in the fading months before the outbreak of war, a line was drawn in the record books, closing a series of long-remembered hard-fought contests, the traditional battlegrounds for many preceding generations of gentlemen cadets.

CHAPTER 11

Mobilisation and the War Years

THE LAST DAYS OF THE SHOP

Unknown to many, in that last year before the war the long debate on amalgamation was ended. In May 1939 the Army Council decided that, after the introduction of compulsory military service the following month, all who qualified for cadetships through the Army Entrance Examination should do six months' training at the Guards Depot, Caterham, before joining the Royal Military Academy Sandhurst, which would open in August 1940. Moreover, the Shop at the outbreak of war would neither become an Officer Cadet Training Unit nor be taken over by the Military College of Science, but would close. Meanwhile, as a gentleman cadet who joined the RMA in January 1939 recalls, the normal training continued.

The SUO kept us all in good order, and one dreadful day he accused us all of having 'idle tiepins' . . . We rode under Nat Kindersley and Sailor Kitcat, cut our fingers in the workshops under Mr Dann, were given a broad view of current events by Messrs Boswell and Taylor, and mapped Woolwich Common and contoured Greenwich Park. We did PT and swam, learned maths, and the organisation of the cavalry division, and discovered how Napoleon took Italy, and Wellington took Napoleon. We suffered or sniggered at the 'snooker boxing', studied French under Costa de Beauregard – chiefly because he looked so natty and had a reputation for telling bawdy stories – and dashed at great speed from place to place to change our clothes. In fact we did all the things that GCs have always done, even to falling out from lunch parade to 'buy a horse' so we could ride in the afternoon.

From early in 1939 the War Office had been calling for more and more officers. Between March and the beginning of July four batches of Shop cadets were commissioned, none having done more than two terms. All that remained was the most recently commissioned batch of 'young officers', who were held back for a month's crash course, and the juniors, who went off to camp before the summer break. The staff got no leave, as short courses for Reserve officers stretched on until the Academy re-

147

assembled on 24 August. When the new 'snookers' arrived the cadet strength was 214. With a declaration of war expected daily, little attempt was made to operate the normal syllabus. Sandbagging, gas training and air-defence precautions became a priority, and all the cadets were enrolled as private soldiers in the Territorial Army in preparation for joining a wartime OCTU. At 1630 hours on 1 September came the order to mobilise.

The cadets were warned, given tea, marched off to hand in rifles, stores, books, etc., instructed to pack their kits, and finally paraded at 1800 hours ready to leave. The MT Section carried them and their kits to the station; the complete blackout increased the difficulties of transport. By 2200 hours they had all left, the last cadets ever to live and work in the Shop, in fact it was the very Shop itself which went down the hill to the Arsenal Station that September evening. During the night and early next day the staff, military and civilian, departed to their mobilisation posts.

As Maurice-Jones adds, 'the Shop, after a life of 198 years, had ceased to exist'.

Their Majesties King George VI and Queen Elizabeth visit the RMC OCTU in 1940.

In contrast, Sandhurst, already chosen to house the amalgamated military academy, was kept full to overflowing throughout the war. In January 1939 there were just over 600 gentlemen cadets under training. By early July all but the junior term had been commissioned. The summer break was devoted to two courses for a total of 700 junior officers of the Territorial Army, and the new term opened with an intake of 271 gentlemen cadets. Then, after a further six weeks, the previous juniors were passed out. Meanwhile, on mobilisation taking place, 550 officers and men of GHQ British Expeditionary Force assembled at the RMC prior to their departure overseas. There was very tight security. Government House became a staging post for the Commander-in-Chief and some of his staff, and it was here that the Commander-in-Chief, Lord Gort, and HRH The Duke of Gloucester stayed on the night before they left for France.

On 4 September, the day after war was declared, the RMC became the Sandhurst OCTU. There were two wings, the 101 Royal Armoured Corps Wing and the 161 Infantry Wing. The Inns of Court Regiment arrived as a complete unit, to start up the RAC Wing, while the RMC infantry cadets formed the nucleus of the Infantry Wing under some of the existing staff. Cadets for the cavalry, machine-gun units or corps were dispersed to OCTUs elsewhere. The Infantry course was sixteen weeks, but the RAC course was extended by another eight weeks to cover tactical and gunnery instruction at Bovington.

Three weeks after the outbreak of war the first batch of officer cadets arrived, mostly straight from university and without any preliminary training. Subsequently all cadets passed through the ranks before joining, and all those destined for the Brigade of Guards were automatically sent to Sandhurst. At the end of October Major General Eastwood handed over to Brigadier Kemp-Welch. His opposite number as Commandant at Woolwich, Major General Philip Neame, VC, was already in post as Deputy Chief of the General Staff, and 'Rusty' Eastwood was appointed to command a division.

Some of the company officers were retained, at least for a time. The Adjutant Captain E.H. Goulburn, Grenadier Guards, was kept back for a year before handing over to Captain H.N. Clowes, Scots Guards, and the Quartermaster Major 'Archie' Sandy continued to work miracles on the administrative side right through the war. One of the biggest problems was finding accommodation for the influx of instructors, drivers and specialists of all kinds, let alone the extra lecture rooms and stores. All the troop horses had been sent off to Melton Mowbray the day after war was declared, and almost overnight the riding schools began to fill up with tanks and motor transport of all kinds. One stable block was converted to house the Administrative Wing, others became lecture rooms and stores. The Married Families Club became a cookhouse and other ranks' mess room. The contractor's shed behind the Library was turned into a miniature range and a model room.

One of the more dramatic moves occurred a little later in the war. For many years the sergeants' mess had been established in the basement of the Old Buildings, in what is now the Academy Club, but it had become overcrowded to an intolerable degree. Having called a mess meeting, the President, Regimental Sergeant Major A.J. Brand, Grenadier Guards, gave the somewhat unusual order that each member was to pick up the chair he was sitting on, or some other piece of mess property, and move straight to the 'New Mess' – the converted stable block below Chapel Square.

In July 1942 the Infantry Wing moved to Mons Barracks, Aldershot, as

Captain H.N. Clowes, Adjutant at Sandhurst in 1940, riding up the steps to the Grand Entrance at the end of a passing-out parade for one of the wartime OCTU courses.

161 (RMC) OCTU, where it remained until the end of the war, with the cadets still wearing the RMC badge. The 100 (RAC) OCTU now came into being, complete with Wireless, Gunnery and Tactical Wings, and the full six months' course took place in and around Sandhurst, with a squad passing out every fortnight. In spite of the intensive nature of the course full use was made of the sports grounds, and a highlight of one cricket season in the middle of the war was a two-day match at Lord's between a Sandhurst XI, half instructors and half cadets, captained by Ronnie Aird, and Pelham Warner's All-England XI. When the RAC OCTU moved to Bovington in November 1945 the 161 OCTU returned to Sandhurst before closing down some nine months later.

Within the shelter of the Sandhurst grounds life during the war years took on an even pattern. Although the main buildings were an easily recognisable target, there is no record of daylight air attack, and as far as can be discovered there were only two serious instances of night bombing

The Royal Armoured Corps OCTU at Sandhurst. The Tank School set up in one of the indoor riding schools, as it was in January 1943.

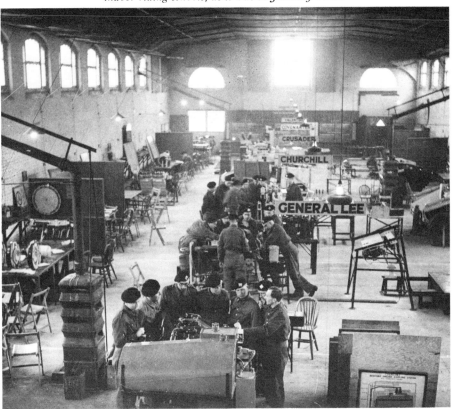

during the whole war, one of which is recalled by an officer who was a cadet in 'B' Company early in 1941 and already a veteran from the campaign of 1940 in France:

On the evening of Wednesday 29 January, after dinner, when most of us were taking coffee, a single bomb was dropped and hit the end of 'C' Block of the New Buildings. It was a bright night and no doubt the lake was a clear landmark for a bomber returning from London. Some cadets were in the habit of going straight back to their rooms after dinner and five of these were killed in 'C' Block that evening. The bomb demolished the end of the wing, and it had not been repaired when I passed out in April.

The second incident occurred towards the end of the war when a land-mine dropped between the two main buildings and not far from Lake House. There were no casualties but many windows were blown out and the effect of the blast stretched as far as the Chapel, where two or three of the stained-glass windows suffered damage. The Quartermaster's figure for the 'total' number of windowpanes that had to be replaced is believed to have been quite expansive! The lake had in fact been drained, if only to satisfy local fears that it was too easily identifiable from the air.

Another kind of aerial assault occurred on the night of 6/7 December 1942 when two parachutists landed on the roof of the Old Buildings and were promptly arrested. They turned out to be two RAF air crew who had baled out from a badly damaged bomber returning from Europe, and the plane crashed shortly afterwards.

Apart from the requirements for officer-cadet training, there were demands for accommodation at Sandhurst to house a variety of special courses, for young officers serving in armoured regiments, for training officers recalled from the Reserve as umpires, for liaison officers' courses, and later in the war to house a wing of the Staff College. An officer sent early in 1940 to the Liaison Wing at Sandhurst, which was housed in Le Marchant House, describes some of the training:

Here were run a number of courses to train subalterns, drawn principally from the Infantry, to be motor contact officers, later called junior liaison officers. Each course was for about twenty officers, and we were put through a kind of miniature staff course so that we had a wide knowledge of Army organisation up to corps level. Motorcycling, a novelty to most of us, formed a considerable part of the course, and in a week or so we were riding cross-country at night without lights over the heathland at the back of the RMC.

In December 1942 the Junior Staff College moved from Oxford into

The Churchill Hall, opened by Mrs Christopher Soames in 1970, viewed from the road leading to Windsor Ride.

The Central Library, showing the main room, originally a gymnasium, and the passage leading to the Marlow Hall which houses the military history collection.

Officer cadets of the RMA Sandhurst in the early post-war period drilling on the New Buildings Square. From the painting by Dennis Flanders. RMA Sandhurst Collection.

Presentation of New Colours by Her Majesty The Queen to the RMA Sandhurst, 30 May 1974. Commanding the parade is the Adjutant, Major J.J. Pope, Coldstream Guards, and in front, facing the microphones, is the Commandant, Major General R.C. Ford. Detail from the painting by Joan Wanklyn.

part of the New Buildings. The large first-floor room under the clock tower became the main lecture room, and separate dining facilities were provided in two huts behind the building. These had been put up immediately before the war as part of the preparations for moving certain branches of the War Office out of London in the event of heavy air attack. These 'Sandhurst' courses lasted four months and continued until the end of March 1946. The 'school solution' for dealing with the accumulated mess funds provided a suitable and memorable ending to the last course – a splendidly organised dance, with breakfast served by candlelight, and other celebrations that continued for several days.

A 'Champion' Company of ATS

One of the ATS officers who served at Sandhurst during the war describes how the girls reacted to their new environment and how the other residents of Sandhurst reacted to them:

Two territorial companies of ATS were posted to Sandhurst early in September 1939. These were the 7th City of London Company and the 1st Surrey Company. The 7th City of London cooks and orderlies worked in the New Buildings, the 1st Surreys in the Old Building, the clerks were spread out through the various offices in the College. . . . Both officers and other ranks were very 'green' as to Army life and ways. Major Sandy, the Quartermaster, was the guide, philosopher and friend. Later in the war, when ATS were permitted to wear Sam Browne belts, within hours of the ACI coming out, the ATS officers were asked to go to Major Sandy's office and were presented with well-polished belts. The officers attending a meeting that afternoon outside the College were the envy of all other ATS officers. It is right to say that all ranks ATS felt it a great honour to serve at Sandhurst . . . and had a great affection for the place.

ATS were accommodated in the other ranks' married quarters . . . The sick bay was suitably housed in No. 9, 'A' Block, but later moved to Lake House. No. 4 The Square was the officers' mess and company office. At the end of 1939 a single company was formed, comprising the 7th City of London Platoon and the 1st Surrey Platoon. This was not very popular . . . To boost *esprit de corps*, Major Sandy arranged that our ATS should wear the red lanyards given before the war to the Champion Cadet Company.

In 1941 the ATS expanded to the Staff College and Minley Manor, and in 1943 made an ATS Group when the posting of drivers further swelled the numbers. The ATS who worked at the Staff College wore the owl badge over their top left pockets. They were proud of this, but not all knew its significance. One of the girls, when asked what it was, looked down and said, 'I fink it's a puthy cat.'

RSM 'Bosom' Brand was another great friend to the ATS and took them for drill once a week on the parade ground, giving the ATS officers a separate drill

His Majesty King George VI inspecting tank crews under instruction during a visit to the RAC OCTU at Sandhurst in May 1943.

session. . . . The ATS joined the cadets for church parade, and one old soldier came each Sunday, bringing with him his weekend guests. One could expect him to be horrified and groan at the sight. However, he was heard to say as the ATS came into the straight for the march-past, 'Here they come, aren't they splendid, much better than the cadets.' One morning 'Bosom' had a blitz on the cadets and really stretched his vocabulary. A cadet later in the day reported to some friends, 'I have just seen "Bosom" drilling the ATS. The most he said to them, with every button on his uniform straining with the effort, was "Ladies, PLEASE pay more attention".'

The Bandmaster decided that each company in the College should choose their own tune with which to march past on Sundays. The ATS chose 'The First Time I Put This Uniform On' in respect for Arthur Sullivan (of Gilbert and Sullivan fame), who was born in the Old Building. The Bandmaster had other ideas, and the ATS found themselves marching past to 'They'd Be Far Better Off in a Home'. . . .

Although it was 'out of bounds' many cadets did get invited to No. 4 The Square

Church Parade at Sandhurst in 1942. The Sandhurst Company Auxiliary Territorial Service marching past Their Majesties The King and Queen.

on Wednesday evenings; two bottles of beer inside the battledress top was the pass. Cadets under training at the Wireless School would line up on the road past the Chapel in their transport, to tune in and 'get on net'. For the first few years of the war a physiotherapist from a Voluntary Aid Detachment of the Red Cross ran the 'Physio' department at the hospital. She lived in the ATS officers' mess. She decided to 'fix' the Wireless School by jamming their wireless sets with her portable diathermy machine. The cadets, having tuned in, were about to move off, when their sets suddenly jammed. Instructors and NCOs ran to and fro trying to locate the mysterious trouble, which vanished as suddenly as it came, then reappeared. The watchers and operator from No. 4 The Square allowed this to happen for about ten minutes, then left it alone. This was repeated for a couple of mornings. The following Wednesday several students from the Wireless School reported for the beer party at No. 4. Mention was made of the trouble the Wireless School seemed to have getting tuned in. The cadets were earnest in their discussion as to what had happened and did not notice winks and knowing smiles. Lord Haw-haw was finally blamed.

157

CHAPTER 12

The New Academy

THE ROYAL MILITARY ACADEMY SANDHURST OPENS

As we have seen, the concept of amalgamating the two colleges had been argued over for more than a century. In the inter-war years Lord Haldane's 1923 Committee and a special sub-committee set up subsequently by the Army Council had both rejected the proposal on the grounds that 'the standard at Sandhurst was too low for Woolwich'. As so often happens, it was on financial grounds that the matter was finally decided. A committee appointed by Duff Cooper, the Financial Secretary to the War Office, argued that through amalgamation an annual saving of £42,000 would be achieved. For a time other factors prevailed, but from this moment the fate of the Shop was sealed.

The detailed planning that was set in motion in December 1938 made rapid progress. In essence the decision was for the new Academy to have an establishment of 732 cadets organised in eight companies. They were all to be on the same syllabus, except only that in mathematics and science the 'Artillery' cadets would be separated from the remainder from the start. Taking into account the cost of building laboratories and other extra accommodation, there would still be substantial savings. Then the war intervened and the files themselves were destroyed in an air-raid.

By January 1946 planning for the 'Post-War Army College' was again being pressed forward. The intention was the same, but post-war conditions, combined with a shortage of materials of all kinds, would inevitably create many difficulties and delay any new building programme. Somehow all the resultant problems, administrative and otherwise, would have to be overcome.

The man chosen as first Commandant RMA Sandhurst was undoubtedly the right man for the job. Major General F.R.G. Matthews, DSO, was appointed in July, and in less than six months the first intake of officer cadets would arrive. Mark Matthews, as he was always known, joined the RMC from Cheltenham College in 1921, and after the two-year course joined the York and Lancaster Regiment. He later transferred to

RMA Sandhurst, 1947. Major General F.R.G. Matthews and H.H. Hardy, the first Commandant and Director of Studies.

the South Wales Borderers on accelerated promotion and commanded the 1st Battalion in the North African campaign before becoming Commandant of the Staff College at Sarafand. In the last two years of the war he commanded infantry brigades in Italy and North-West Europe, and immediately before coming to Sandhurst was GOC 53 (Welsh) Division.

The War Office directive, issued at the end of July 1946, briefly stated that the RMA Sandhurst would open on 3 January 1947 as the chief means of training cadets for regular commissions in the Army. The course would be for eighteen months, consisting of a broad education based on a foundation of general military training, and the syllabus would have the object of achieving the following ends:

The development of the cadet's character, his powers of leadership, and a high standard of individual and collective discipline. An understanding of the art of command and elements of military discipline and the means whereby a high morale can be achieved and sustained. The inculcation of the means by which an officer can keep himself and those under his command mentally alert and physically fit. An enthusiasm sufficient to ensure the officer's own further unaided study of military subjects and general world affairs.

On 4 January 1947, the Commandant addressed the first intake of 328 officer cadets. This is part of what he said:

You . . . are making history today . . . You are in the same position as those cadets who went to the Royal Military Academy, Woolwich, in 1741, and to the Royal Military College, Sandhurst, in 1799. Their traditions have stood the ravages of time. I want you to realise that on your shoulders will lie the future tone, tradition and general moral behaviour of this Academy.

Three weeks later the Chief of the Imperial General Staff, Field Marshal the Viscount Montgomery, visited the Academy. His address to the cadets was on 'Leadership and Morale'. He then spoke at some length on the importance of their learning languages, and in particular Russian, which in future was to be taught at Sandhurst.

The ranks of the academic staff were now beginning to fill up, and in spite of the difficulty of obtaining up-to-date textbooks in sufficient quantities, work on the various courses was well advanced. To begin with, the Academy was organised on a two-college basis. Old College was commanded by Lieutenant Colonel R.E. Goodwin and New College by Lieutenant Colonel D.A.K.W. Block. The first intake was formed into four companies, each named after a famous battle honour, Blenheim and Waterloo in the Old, and Marne and Somme in the New Buildings. The arrival of a further 200 cadets in May completed the college organisations with Dettingen, Inkerman, Ypres and Gaza Companies. Distinguishing colours for each college, as for instance the colour of the lanyard worn with battledress, had already been decided on: red for Old College, representing the scarlet worn by the pre-1914 Army, blue for New College, and gold for Victory College, which was formed with the arrival of Intake 2 in August. The first commander of Victory College was Lieutenant Colonel G.A.E. Peyton, and the companies were named after the Second World War battle honours, Alamein, Normandy, Rhine and Burma. The cadet strength was now 964, and the cadets of New and Victory Colleges had to double up in the New Buildings.

At Academy Headquarters there was no Assistant Commandant but a Chief Instructor, Colonel M.S.K. Maunsell, alongside whom was the Director of Studies, H.H. Hardy. 'H.H.', as he was always known, was a former headmaster of Cheltenham College and later Shrewsbury School. Commissioned before the Great War, he served with the Royal Warwickshire Regiment in France and on the staff of the Fifth Army. Later in 1939, while still at Shrewsbury, he was appointed to the Committee on the Supply of Officers, and on retiring in 1944 held an appointment at the

RSM A.J. Brand taking a squad in Communication Drill.

Admiralty. The complex administrative affairs of the Academy were in the hands of Colonel C.G. Robins and two quartermasters, the senior of whom was Major 'Happy' Havilland. Outside the college organisation there were specialist training wings: Drill and Weapon Training under the Adjutant, Major the Earl of Cathcart, Driving and Maintenance under Major Wicks, Fitness and Hygiene under Major Tresawna, and the Signal Communications Wing under Major McGill. Under the Director of Studies there were two faculties, Science and Mathematics, and Modern Subjects and Languages, with a head to each of the four departments. Four of these key members of the staff had taught their subjects at the Shop: the two Heads of Faculty, Dr Stevenson and K.C. Boswell, together with G.R. Sisson (Mathematics) and J.W. Taylor (Modern Subjects). The other two Heads of Departments were G.F. Dixon (Science) and W. Lough (Modern Languages). The establishment of officers and senior civilian staff may be summarised as follows: Academy Headquarters, 22; specialist wings, 11; medical officers, 2; chaplains, 2; librarians, 3. The three colleges had a total of 78 officers, and the senior civilian staff in the two faculties numbered 63.

The spread of war experience among the staff as a whole was impressive. Many of the officers had held high 'wartime' rank, and the civilian lecturing staff had been recruited from recently demobilised graduates or those who had taken their degrees after war service in the Forces. The Regimental Sergeant Major, A.J. Brand, had enlisted in the Grenadier Guards in 1915 and within three years, at the age of twenty, had risen to the rank of Company Sergeant Major. He joined the RMC in 1938, and during the war some 15,000 cadets passed through his hands. On and off the parade ground he held the respect and affection of staff and cadets alike, but woe betide any who failed to meet his standards.

As was traditional, the drill staff was found by the Brigade of Guards, and including specialist instructors, the number of warrant officers and sergeants on the establishment came to well over a hundred, with more than fifty corps and regiments being represented. Amongst the 'College Servants', and the name has long survived, were a number who had given over forty years loyal and devoted service to the RMC since coming out of the Forces at the end of the Great War, while Mr W.C. Taylor, a cook, had joined the year the South African War broke out at the age of fourteen. Of the ladies, Mrs Parrant in the laundry could claim thirty-nine years' service at Sandhurst.

With the eyes of the world on the newly established Academy, important visitors began to arrive in increasing numbers and with ever greater frequency. Previously Sandhurst had enjoyed a degree of the privacy that Le Marchant had sought in his choice of the site. Now it had become 'on the circuit' for many visiting foreign dignitaries. The earliest of such visits was by a delegation from the Praesidium of the Supreme Soviet which was headed by M.U.V. Zuznetsov and which included M.M. Gromov, Colonel General of Aviation. From America came the first of the distinguished high-ranking US Army officers to deliver the Kermit Roosevelt Lecture. This exchange of lecturers had been established shortly after the end of the Second World War at the suggestion and through the generosity of Mrs Kermit Roosevelt in memory of her late husband, who had served in the British Army in both World Wars.

AN HISTORIC OCCASION

In June 1947 there was a royal occasion that truly marked the birth of the new Academy, the presentation of Colours by His Majesty King George VI, who was accompanied by Her Majesty the Queen and both the royal princesses. Unfortunately the weather broke just as the parade started, but in spite of the rain all went smoothly. The following cadets were chosen for special duties: Ensign to the King's Colour, Officer Cadet Lance Corporal G.C. Anderson; Ensign to the Regimental Colour, Officer Cadet D.A. Henderson; Escort to the Colours, Officer Cadet Lance Corporal M.A.P. Mitchell, Officer Cadet B.S. Read and Officer Cadet A.C.H. Price;

the King's Orderlies, Officer Cadet C.W. Huxley and Officer Cadet I. Grainger.

In accordance with long-established custom the royal party walked the length of the King's Walk to the dais on the edge of the parade ground. After the Royal Salute, His Majesty inspected the battalion drawn up in line. The flank companies then formed inwards and the two college commanders brought forward the Colours and placed them on piled drums in the centre of the open square. The consecration service was conducted by the Chaplain General, Canon Hughes, assisted by the Reverend Davidson, Deputy Chaplain General, and the Chaplain of the Academy, the Reverend Battersby. His Majesty then addressed the cadets, and concluded with the following words:

Above all, remember that the career which you have undertaken is one of great unselfishness. Your Colours, by their consecration, may remind you of the supreme example of unselfishness which the world has seen, and your motto, 'Serve to Lead', may teach you that only by emulating such an example can you each hope to play your part as a commander of men.

After the Commandant's reply in words of loyalty and humble duty, the parade continued with the march-past in slow and quick time, the advance in review order, a final Royal Salute, and three cheers for His Majesty. The Colours were then marched off and placed in the dining room of the New Buildings, where the royal party were to take luncheon with members of the staff, guests and officer cadets from both colleges.

When the time came for the royal party to return to Windsor, His Majesty exercised the royal prerogative of driving along the King's Walk. Here the whole Academy was assembled to give three cheers for the royal family – cheers that echoed back from the great façade of Wyatt's building, repeating their message of loyalty and affection.

THE PATTERN OF INSTRUCTION

In August, with the arrival of another intake, 360 strong, the full pattern of the eighteen-month course took shape. The senior batch now occupied its proper place under the traditional system of cadet government, providing the under officers and other cadet appointments within the full college structure. This long-established system was not only a projection of the normal military chain of command but placed at successive levels a responsibility on all senior cadets for maintaining set standards of discipline and behaviour. All cadets from the day they joined were introduced to the concept of responsibility. The more experienced cadets had to guide and take control of others only months younger than themselves, with each learning from the other essential lessons in leadership that soon must be demonstrated in front of the men entrusted to their command. It is a system which has immense value.

As in pre-war days, the basic unit was the company, but when it came to the educational part of the syllabus, cadets had to be placed into classes according to their ability and the Arm of the Service they hoped to join. In the words of the directive, the aim was 'a proper balanced educational background, so that after leaving the Academy the cadet may advance progressively to full officer status'. After the first term cadets destined for the more technical corps would have to specialise in certain subjects 'to ensure that subsequent training is not unduly prolonged', and the minimum passing-out standard would be that of 'an intermediate degree in the University Science Course'. Other cadets would have a choice, outside the obligatory subjects, of making a special study selected from the military history, modern or scientific parts of the curriculum. Teaching was to be on university lines with directed private study.

The object of the military training was to give a basic military education common to all Arms, providing the cadet with the background for further study. Particular emphasis was to be given to the qualities required by leaders in peace and war, the elements of morale and the importance of inter-service co-operation.

The programmed time over the whole course was equally divided between the military and educational subjects. Two comparisons show some of the emphasis. The time allotted for drill, PT and organised games together roughly equated with the 18 per cent given to the obligatory course in science and mathematics; or to take the single subjects, the 5 per cent of the total periods given for teaching administration was matched by a similar allocation for language-training in French, German or Russian, outside the additional periods allocated where one of these languages was taken as an optional special subject.

THE COMPETITIVE SPIRIT

Away from the parade ground and the classrooms there was much to keep everyone busy. With an almost inexhaustible supply of talent amongst the staff, the conventional games and sports were well organised and flourishing. Some activities, of themselves attracting a number of cadets, were proving difficult to start up so soon after the end of the war. Four teams in modern pentathlon were under training, and many cadets were anxious to learn to ride, but the stables were empty and the number of horses that could be hired was very limited. The Flying Club, with over 70 members, had a single glider and two others loaned by the RA Aero Club, and the

Presentation by cadets from West Point of a plaque bearing the badge of the United States Military Academy.

Sailing Club's 160 members had to make do with three ex-German Olympics and a 12-foot National dinghy presented by Major the Earl Cathcart, but there were plans to double the size of the fleet before the following season. Other clubs in an early state of development catered for the rifle or shotgun enthusiast and those who sought the challenge of rock-climbing and potholing. Also popular were the Automobile Club and the Motorcycle Club, both unfortunately restricted in their activities by the petrol cuts.

To complete the list at a less active level were societies and clubs for those interested in photography and painting, as well as music or chess and even ornithology. Soon the number of sports and activities became even more comprehensive, as parachuting, skiing and offshore cruising were added, together with a Russian Circle and a well-supported Dramatic Society, to name only a few. Progressively the emphasis turned towards the

165

more active pursuits coming within the province of 'Adventure Training', which included major expeditions during long recesses to such distant places as Nepal, Iceland, Norway and Ethiopia.

During the spring and summer of 1947 the Champion Company Competition was restarted, following closely the pre-war pattern. At this time all the major sports were included, but these were eliminated five years later. The most important event remained the Company Drill Competition. The King George V Banner had been in sanctuary in the Chapel since 1939, and in November 1947 a special service was arranged at which General HRH The Duke of Gloucester re-presented the Banner.

The following spring the Bugle Competition was reintroduced at the Athletic Sports, bringing another link with pre-war traditions. At the same time two annual athletic matches were established: a pentangular match between Sandhurst, St Cyr, the Ecole Polytechnique and the Belgian and Dutch military academies; and a triangular match with Dartmouth and Cranwell. Soon other contacts were arranged with the military academies of Western Europe and the United States through exchange visits of parties of cadets, and in this country regular annual

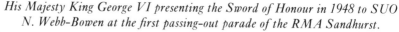

His Majesty King George VI presenting the Sword of Honour in 1948 to SUO N. Webb-Bowen at the first passing-out parade of the RMA Sandhurst.

166

fixtures in the major sports with the cadet colleges of the other Services became important features of the Sandhurst calendar.

HIS MAJESTY AND THE SOVEREIGN'S PARADE

After two exacting years launching the new Academy Major General Matthews was appointed GOC in Hong Kong and handed over to Major General H.C. Stockwell, CB, CBE, DSO. 'Hughie' Stockwell had been educated at Marlborough and the RMC, before joining the Royal Welch Fusiliers in 1923. Immediately prior to arriving at Sandhurst he had been GOC 6th Airborne Division during the last ten difficult months of the Mandate in Palestine. A former commandant of a commando school and a fully qualified parachutist, General Stockwell was a fine athlete, with Sandhurst blues for cricket and hockey and a half-blue in rugger to his credit, as well as being a keen yachtsman and rider to hounds. Like his predecessor, he was destined to make a vital contribution to the development of the pattern of life and work at the Academy.

Soon after General Stockwell's arrival His Majesty the King took the passing-out parade for Intake 1; the date, 14 July 1948. This memorable and inspiring occasion took place in bright sunshine before a great gathering of several thousand visitors, and the twelve companies at full strength carried out the time-honoured ceremonial with an impressive precision. Commanding the parade was the Adjutant Major C. Earle, Grenadier Guards, with the Assistant Adjutant Captain D.A. Lambert, Irish Guards, as second in command. For Regimental Sergeant Major Brand it was his last parade before retiring. The number of officer cadets on parade was 1,222. The King's Colour was carried by Junior Under Officer Mitchell, the Regimental Colour by Junior Under Officer Homan, and the King George V Banner by Officer Cadet Sergeant Harpur. His Majesty's address, given after the advance in review order, contained the following passages:

It is just over a year ago that I gave you your new Colours and I am glad to be here again today to see a passing-out parade which includes for the first time the future officers of every branch of the Army. It is now for others to take on the responsibilities and opportunities of the senior term. A standard has been set, and it is for those of you who are remaining at Sandhurst to equal or to excel it, since on your combined efforts and on your individual conduct will depend the honour of this great Academy.

His Majesty then presented the Sword of Honour to Senior Under Officer Webb-Bowen and the King's Medal to Senior Under Officer Hicks. Then Regimental Sergeant Major Brand was called forward to receive the

Medal of the Royal Victorian Order. The parade was now drawing to an end, and soon the seniors were marching up the steps into the Grand Entrance, followed by the Adjutant on his charger. Then the Champion Company (Inkerman), escorting the King George V Banner, marched past His Majesty, exercising their privilege of marching off before the remainder of the battalion.

Before lunch senior members of the staff were presented to His Majesty in the large upstairs anteroom of the officers' mess in the New Buildings. In conversation His Majesty remarked that he wished to mark the occasion by naming the parade in future 'The King's Parade' and the Champion Company 'The King's Company'. At this the Adjutant, Charles Earle, stepped forward and with due respect begged to remind His Majesty that he already had a King's Company which was found by the Grenadier Guards. King George did not hesitate for a moment: 'Then it shall be "The Sovereign's Parade" and "The Sovereign's Company".' Standing nearby were the Secretary of State for War, the Right Honourable Emanuel Shinwell, and several members of the Army Council, and over a glass of sherry the matter was settled on the spot by an order in council. Within minutes a telegram notifying His Majesty's commands, dictated by the Adjutant over the guardroom telephone, was on its way to the War Office.

Environmental Matters

In the early days of the RMA Sandhurst important visitors were proudly shown a large model of the buildings and grounds of the 'Sandhurst of the future'. How long it survived as a reminder of the foresight and expectations of Mark Matthews and his dedicated team of planners is not recorded, but it must soon have become clear that the 'future' was a long way ahead. With the months and years slipping by, this master plan, designed to provide essential support for present tasks and a proper insurance for many years to come, suffered the inevitable results of the post-war shortages and stringent economies on building programmes which, combined with the upward spiral of costs, brought postponements and cancellations to all but some day-to-day maintenance and minor works services.

Under what might almost be described as siege conditions, improvisation had to be resorted to and much use made of temporary structures. The most urgent need was for extra cadet accommodation. A Royal Engineer unit was brought in from Germany, and in a matter of weeks a hutted 'camp' began to rise behind the New Buildings, spreading back towards King's Ride and the rifle ranges. Some of these temporary buildings were allocated as bachelor officers' quarters and as offices and extra classrooms, but the majority took the overflow of cadets from the two colleges sharing the New Buildings. Only now, years after the Departments of Science and Mathematics moved from the hospital blocks on Windsor Ride into the new science building, the Faraday Hall, and the long-awaited Victory College was finally completed, has it been possible to give up many of these temporary huts. Following are the dates for the building of the 'New Sandhurst':

1957	Central Boiler House	1977	Extension to Sergeants' Mess
1958	Other Ranks' Quarters	1978	Oman Hall (Sports Centre,
1959	Sandhurst Hall		opened by HE the
	Married Quarters for Other		Ambassador of the Sultanate
	Ranks (243 built over the		of Oman)
	next 17 years)		Skill at Arms and Signal
1960	Sergeants' Mess		Training Wings
	Swimming Bath		New Soldiers' Mess
1961	Faraday Hall, with Narrien		
	Library	*Under Construction :*	
1969	Academy Headquarters		Barrack Block for
1970	East Building, for Victory		Demonstration Company
	College		Extension to Junior Ranks
	Churchill Hall (opened by		Club
	Mrs Christopher Soames)		
1976	Physiotherapy and Dental Centre		

A Guest Night in the Sergeants' Mess in 1952, showing the dining room in part of the converted stables.

Since the end of the war a number of married officers' quarters have been built on Barossa.

It is not only through the names of many of these buildings that we are reminded of the foundations of the present Academy. In the grounds stand Queen Victoria's statue and the Memorial to the Prince Imperial, both brought from Woolwich. Similarly, in the corridors of Old College are honour boards listing the winners of the Pollock and Tombs prizes and Distinguished Officers of the Engineers, Royal Artillery and Royal Signals. Portraits, prints and Paul Sandby's paintings from the Shop hang alongside similar items presented to the RMC, and many of the sports trophies are regularly displayed on guest nights.

From the start the Central Library took on the responsibility for maintaining a representative exhibition of these paintings, military prints and historic relics. This display was considerably enhanced and enlarged by a most generous presentation by the late Colonel C. de W. Crookshank of his personal collection of military prints, *objets d'art* and relics. Meanwhile India had obtained her independence, and to provide a permanent home for the hundreds of items presented in memory of the regiments of the old Indian Army, and of the generations of British officers sent out from Sandhurst and the Shop, it was decided to establish an Indian Army Memorial Room in the old chapel behind the Grand Entrance of the Old Buildings.

It was soon apparent that a curator was required to compete with these ever-growing 'museum' responsibilities. The first to be appointed was Lieutenant Colonel Boultbee, late 7th Light Cavalry, and after a few years he was succeeded by Lieutenant Colonel Appelby. From these early beginnings came the concept of a National Army Museum, soon to be officially established under the inspired direction of General, later Field Marshal, Sir Gerald Templer. A Cavalry and Disbanded Irish Regiments' Section was opened in basement rooms behind Old College in 1954, and the main collection was given a temporary home in one of the riding schools off Chapel Square, while funds were raised for building its permanent home next to the Royal Hospital, Chelsea. Sandhurst's own collection, depicting the history of the pre-war colleges and the present academy, has meanwhile come under the expert and enthusiastic direction of its curator, Dr Tony Heathcote.

THE CHAPEL AND ITS MEMORIALS

A committee set up in 1945 to plan a memorial in the Chapel to the officers who had given their lives in the Second World War brought together several of those who had been involved in rebuilding the Chapel itself –

Sandhurst entertains officers and cadets of St Cyr, the French Military Academy, after Exercise 'La Madelon', May 1963. Watching the Beating of Retreat are (centre) the Commandant, Major General J.H. Mogg, and to his right Dr K. Ingham (the Director of Studies) and Mrs Ingham.

Scientific expedition in south-east Ethiopia led by Captain J. Blashford-Snell. Sandhurst cadets crossing a river on a sectional ferry made by Daimlers. In striped shirt, Richard Snailham, Lecturer in Modern Subjects.

A group of stained-glass windows, designed by Lawrence Lee, placed in the Chapel in memory of Field Marshals who have reached that rank since the beginning of the Second World War.

Harry Blackburne, A.C. Martin and Sir Bertie Fisher. This memorial, they felt, should not be limited to commemorating cadets from the pre-war colleges but ought to be truly comprehensive so as to include officers from all over the Commonwealth and Empire, many of whom had been trained at Sandhurst during the war. In April 1947 word was received from 'The White Train', in which the King was touring South Africa, that His Majesty had approved the proposal that the memorial should take the following form: a Roll of Honour, containing the names of all commissioned officers of the British Commonwealth Armies who gave their lives in the Second World War; oak pews to furnish the main body of the Chapel, which would bear the carved crests or badges of regiments and corps; and a new organ and screen, which was to be the particular memorial to the Indian Army.

Major General Matthews' appeal for funds initially went to the Colonels and Colonels Commandant of Corps and Regiments, and the following incident typifies the generous and spontaneous response. The day after the letters were posted the Librarian, who had been appointed Honorary Secretary to the Chapel Council, was dealing with the morning mail when a visitor was announced. This was Colonel E.E.J. Moore, a former Adjutant of the RMC and Colonel of the Royal Inniskilling Fusiliers, who had come in person to hand over a cheque for his Regiment's pew, with the apt words of the motto, 'Primus in Indis'. The work of carving over 220 badges into the new oak pews was carried out by three extremely experienced craftsmen over the next two and a half years.

Meanwhile, owing to the partition of India, there was difficulty in raising funds for the new organ and screen, and it was only through the generous response of many individuals, and more especially the officers' associations, together with donations from the two governments, that the work was completed. The architect for this memorial, which incorporated the seventy-four badges of the old Indian Army, was Sir Hugh Casson. In October 1950 these memorials were dedicated by the Reverend Canon F.L. Hughes, the Chaplain General, in the presence of HRH The Duke of Gloucester and representatives of every corps and regiment of the British Army and the old Indian Army and of many Commonwealth regiments.

The production of the Roll of Honour took considerably longer and could never have been achieved without the wholehearted co-operation of the War Graves Commission. The listing of nearly 20,000 entries for officers of the British and Dominion Armies and colonial forces, by their corps and regiments, took over three years. The design, embellishment and inscribing were then entrusted to Miss Elizabeth Friedlander, and the book was bound by Mr Roger Powell of the Royal College of Art. The

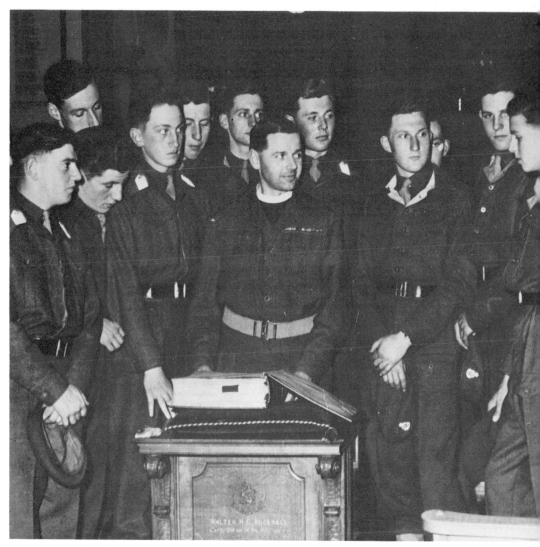

The Chaplain, the Reverend G.W. Battersby, talking to officer cadets of Intake I in the Chapel in January 1947.

dedication of the Roll of Honour took place in October 1956 and was conducted by the Reverend Canon Pike, the Chaplain General, in the presence of Her Majesty Queen Elizabeth the Queen Mother, TRH The Duke and Duchess of Gloucester, the Princess Royal and the Duchess of Kent, and representatives from the whole of the British Army and every part of the Commonwealth.

In 1958 an appeal fund was established by the Commandant, Major General Urquhart, to provide for the continuing beautification of the

Chapel and the maintenance of its memorials. Through the generous response of corps and regiments the original concept of installing stained-glass windows throughout the Chapel has at last been made possible. The four large windows in the nave have been completed, and those in the Chapel of Remembrance that were damaged during the war have been replaced. The design and execution of these windows is by Lawrence Lee, a past Master of the Worshipful Company of Glaziers, and well known for his work in Coventry Cathedral. Above the west door is a further example of Mr Lee's work, a group of three windows in memory of the late King George VI. In more recent years the Chapel Council has decided to commemorate those distinguished officers who have reached the rank of Field Marshal since the start of the Second World War and to reserve the clerestory windows for this purpose.

Of the many other memorials introduced into the Chapel in the last thirty years, two are of particular interest, the large cross hanging in the apse behind the altar, which was presented by the Staff College, and the memorial commemorating the whole history of the Shop and Addiscombe, known as the 'Woolwich Corner'. Both have been designed by John Hayward. Into the preservation and beautification of the Royal Memorial Chapel, Sandhurst, have gone much thought, careful planning and the dedicated work of some of the finest artists and craftsmen in the country.

Here mention should also be made of the Roman Catholic Chapel. This is situated on the first floor of the Old Buildings, in what was originally the No. 2 lecture room. The conversion was under the direction of Colonel Guy Elwes, and the Chapel was opened in December 1948 by His Eminence the Archbishop of Westminster, Cardinal Griffin. The fourteen murals depicting the Way of the Cross are the work of Miss Stella Schmolle, who towards the end of the war was a member of the ATS Company at Sandhurst. Since these early days much has been done to continue the whole process of improving and beautifying the Chapel, and in recent years the sanctuary has been completely redesigned. Amongst the many gifts to the Chapel of Christ the King is a magnificent paschal candlestick presented in 1966 in memory of the officers of the Staff College who gave their lives in the service of their country. The twenty-fifth anniversary of the opening was celebrated by a special service conducted by Cardinal Heenan and with the first chaplain, the Reverend Sidney Lescher, and all of his successors present.

CHAPTER 13

The Pattern of Progress

VIVAT REGINA

In the early morning of 6 February 1952 the country learnt of the death of King George VI, and a broadcast announcement was made that the Sovereign's Parade, which was due to be held the same day, was cancelled. The award of the Gold Medal and the Sword of Honour was made privately in the Library by the Commandant, Major General Dawnay, in a simple ceremony with only the two cadets and their parents present.

As Princess Elizabeth, the new Sovereign had visited Sandhurst on a number of occasions; now 50 of the Sovereign's Company were to march in the procession at her Coronation and 459 officer cadets would line the route in Parliament Square, alongside a similar number of cadets from Dartmouth and Cranwell. On the Friday before the Coronation all three contingents assembled at Sandhurst for rehearsals. On the Sunday, in brilliant weather, a drumhead service was held on Old College Square at which the Chaplain General, Canon Victor Pike, preached on the spiritual significance of the Coronation, calling on all 'to dedicate themselves, even as the Queen herself was to do, to the service of God and Country'.

The weather on Tuesday 2 June 1953 was cold and wet, a fact that is barely mentioned by those on parade. Major V.F. Erskine Crum, the Adjutant at Sandhurst, was in command of the 900 cadets lining the route in Parliament Square and wrote:

Reveille was at 0220 hours, and we left Camberley Station at 0430. We detrained at Vauxhall and marched to Millbank Barracks for breakfast. At 0800 we marched off with the Kneller Hall Band, just as the last of the cars carrying VIPs to the Abbey had cleared our route. We were in position by 0830 and settled down in time for the arrival of the first procession, that of the Lord Mayor. . . . From then until we finally marched off at about 1445 hours time flew. It was the unanimous feeling of all on parade that they would gladly have remained for many hours longer, to see again the pomp and ceremony which made the day.

The Sovereign's Company had left the Academy at 9 a.m. by bus. Senior

Under Officer N.H. Cantlie writes: 'With the assistance of a police escort we arrived in good time at our debussing point in Buckingham Palace Road and marched to our assembly area outside the Palace.' This part of the procession formed up at twelve o'clock, and the Sandhurst cadets were immediately in front of the Honourable Artillery Company.

While we were standing to attention for the Royal Salute of forty-one guns, the rain started in earnest and the guardsmen lining the route put on their grey capes, much to the disappointment of the crowd. However, in spite of the weather, we enjoyed our haversack lunches. At half past one we stepped off down Birdcage Walk and into Parliament Square, past the Sandhurst contingent which was lining the route there, and with silent well-wishing swung off down Whitehall into St James's Street, to halt eventually in Piccadilly, close to Hyde Park Corner.

Rehearsal for the officer cadets of all three Services detailed for ceremonial duties at the Coronation of Her Majesty Queen Elizabeth II, June 1953.

The crowd, thinking that the procession had started, became impatient at the delay, and wondered why we were waiting. 'Procession, quick march.' We were off at last.

The route lay through the park to Marble Arch and via Regent Street back to the Admiralty Arch and up the Mall to reach the park again.

We halted near the Serpentine, and after marching off and casing the King George V Banner, we embussed and started back to Sandhurst. Perhaps the thought uppermost in our minds as we took off our belts and sank into our seats, tired but happy, was that in the coming years we shall remember with pride how we represented Sandhurst in the Coronation Procession of Queen Elizabeth II.

A PEAK PERIOD

In 1952 the British Army was at its post-war peak of 440,000, all ranks, half being National Servicemen or on the recently introduced three-year Short Service Engagement. Although the fighting in Korea was soon to be halted, the situations in Malaya, the Middle East and Kenya continued to make heavy demands over and above Britain's NATO commitments in Europe. The demand for officers continued unabated, and Sandhurst remained very much in the public eye. Each year brought a succession of important visitors and noteworthy occasions. The Commandant in 1954

Left *Cabaret time at the Coronation Ball held in the Gymnasium.*

Right *C.J.S. Bonington climbing in the Avon Gorge in 1955. A prominent member of the Mountaineering and Exploration Club, he was commissioned into the Royal Tank Regiment in December 1955.*

was Major General Hobbs, a former winner of the Sword and the Tombs Medal at the Shop and a Rugby international.

In March HRH Prince Edward, Duke of Kent, joined Alamein Company with Intake 15. He was a junior under officer in his senior term and won the Sir James Moncrieff Grierson Prize for languages. At the end of the eighteen-month course he was commissioned in the Royal Scots Greys. Thirteen years later he returned as an instructor and for twelve months served in Victory College with Rhine Company.

In May a finely executed bronze bust of General Eisenhower was presented to the Academy by Mr George Sands and accepted by the Right Honourable Anthony Head, Secretary of State for War. His Excellency the American Ambassador inspected the parade, and the unveiling ceremony was performed by Mrs Winthrop Aldrich.

The Sovereign's Parade that summer was taken by Field Marshal the Viscount Montgomery in the presence of HRH The Duchess of Kent and Princess Alexandra. In his usual forceful manner he spoke of leadership and comradeship, 'essentials [that] are nourished by our regimental system'. During the summer recess a contingent of Sandhurst cadets took part, for the first time, in the Edinburgh Tattoo.

That autumn the visitors to the Academy included General Rajendrasinhji, Commander-in-Chief Indian Army, HRH General Sir

179

Kiran Rana, Commander-in-Chief the Nepalese Army, and a full Academy parade marked the visit of His Imperial Majesty The Emperor of Ethiopia, the gallant and greatly respected Haile Selassie.

Owing to an adjustment of the terms the winter Sovereign's Parade took place in February 1955, instead of the previous December, and *The Wish Stream* reported that seventy-seven cadets and seven of the staff enjoyed the excellent facilities of Kitzbühel during the recess. The same issue published a contribution from Officer Cadet C.J.S. Bonington of a New Year climbing party in north Wales, and later in the year Brigadier Sir John Hunt gave an informal talk to the Mountaineering and Exploration Club on Everest.

During the summer term HM King Hussein of Jordan took the salute at a parade. This was a visit of some significance as he returned in January 1959 to attend the course as a member of Rhine Company.

HER MAJESTY PRESENTS NEW COLOURS

Over the first ten years more than 5,000 cadets had been commissioned from the RMA Sandhurst, and 1957 was marked by Her Majesty presenting new Colours. In her address to the cadets the Queen spoke of the changing nature of modern warfare, which was bringing reductions to the armed forces of the Crown, while their responsibilities would be no less onerous than in the past. In conclusion she reminded her audience of the great traditions to which they were the heirs, 'built by those who served

Her Majesty The Queen presenting New Colours in June 1957.

and studied here before you upon the firm foundations of unselfishness, heroism and self-sacrifice'.

After the parade Her Majesty went first to the Central Library to view her portrait by Leonard Boden (which now hangs in the officers' mess) and then visited the Chapel, before lunching in Old College. The parade itself, a truly brilliant and memorable occasion, is recorded in a painting by Major Peter Hutchins, then commanding Marne Company, which he generously presented for display in the Library.

This was the year when the winner of the Sword of Honour, Senior Under Officer A.D.W. Abbot-Anderson, became the first Sandhurst cadet to win the Queen's Medal for the champion shot of the Army at Bisley. At the same meeting Quartermaster Sergeant Instructor Atkinson, a member of the Weapon Training staff, won the coveted Army Hundred Cup. In the field of academic studies a new prize was instituted, the Earl Wavell Memorial Prize for military history, the award going to Junior Under Officer R. Holworthy.

Over recent years the military history section in the Library had been expanding rapidly. At the end of the war, when the RMA and RMC libraries were brought together, it was found that many of the Shop books had been ruined by damp and the combined catalogue listed only 8,000 volumes. By 1958 this number had reached about 35,000 volumes and the annual number of issues exceeded 30,000, a third of which were connected with the study of military history. This section was now concentrated in the Commonwealth Room, a move that had been made possible by the construction of a small annex for administrative offices which included a small bindery. It was indeed a matter of some satisfaction to the Librarian that this modest addition of four small rooms added on to the old gymnasium was the first new construction in support of the teaching facilities at Sandhurst for twenty years.

MORE SPORTING ACTIVITIES

The Commandant from November 1956 to January 1960 was Major General Urquhart. His achievements at the Shop have already been mentioned, and much of his service during and after the war had been in Combined Operations. His DSO was won on the Normandy beaches when, as Commander Royal Engineers of 3 Division, he had personally directed the work of all the Royal Engineer units involved in the assault phase of the landing on the left of the British sector. Looking back at the sporting activities of the late 1950s, one cannot doubt that the improved facilities and many successes reflect the enthusiastic interest and support of 'Tiger' Urquhart himself. In the major sports there were full fixture lists in term

The Commandant, Major General Urquhart, congratulating SUO A.D.W. Abbot-Anderson on his winning the Queen's Medal at Bisley in July 1957.

time and BAOR tours during the recess. Athletics flourished, and during the summer term there were over a dozen matches.

Sailing became more popular than ever, and *Robbe* (Baltic 100 sq. m. class) was out every weekend of the season, with long cruises throughout the recess. Through the generosity of the Nuffield Trust a new 30-foot yawl, the *Wish Stream*, was built, and two Fireflies had been donated, bringing the number of dinghies in the club up to eight. In 1958 Sandhurst had six pairs in the Devizes to Westminster canoe race. The conditions were quite appalling, with snow and sleety rain. Redmayne and Turner finished fourth, and another Sandhurst crew eighth, among the sixteen pairs who finished out of sixty starters. Other cadets, members of the Mountaineering and Exploration Club, were testing their endurance and skills on weekend climbing and potholing, with longer expeditions out of term time.

This was a period when the combined RMA Sandhurst and Staff College Saddle Club had forty-two horses on the ration strength, and the Polo Club was providing practice facilities for over twenty cadets, of whom eight played on a regular rota basis at Cowdray. In the Army Pentathlon Championship, Sandhurst continued to enter four teams, while the fencing team won the Southern Command and came second in the Army Team

His Majesty King Hussein inspects the Parade on the occasion of his visit to the RMA Sandhurst in June 1955. The Commandant is Major General R.G.S. Hobbs.

Championship, besides doing particularly well at the Royal Tournament. In rifle-shooting sixteen cadets were entered for the Army Championships, and the team won all but two of their matches, including the one against Cranwell. The tables were turned in the annual small-bore match, with an easy win for Cranwell – a result that the Sandhurst captain of shooting felt reflected an advantage Cranwell gained from having a three-year course.

The opportunities for sport and recreation were almost unlimited, and the sports soon included orienteering and sub-aqua activities. It was indeed a golden age for the 'gladiators', although some might say that too much emphasis was being given to outside events and fixtures.

A SEARCH FOR SOLUTIONS

In 1959, in the aftermath of the Suez débâcle, a decision was taken that National Service should be phased out and that within five years Britain's armed forces would consist entirely of volunteers – a policy that was designed 'to secure substantial reductions in expenditure and manpower'. The plans were that the all-Regular Army should be 165,000 strong, which was less than half the numbers serving when the Government's plans were formulated, but owing to the continuing demands for troops in Malaya, Cyprus and Aden, and later Borneo, the cutback had to be halted

at around 180,000 to cover all these emergencies. Nevertheless, the disbandment and amalgamation of units, combined with the uncertainty of the future, had caused many officers to leave the Service or seek early retirement, and if anything, the demand for young officers had been increased. Among the economy measures Eaton Hall was closed and Mons Officer Cadet School took on the training of all short-service commissioned officers, passing out fifty-one courses between July 1961 and August 1972.

Meanwhile the Sandhurst course had been under close and almost continuous scrutiny. The original course had been based on a total of just over 2,000 programmed periods, and with changes in emphasis this was reduced to about 1,650, with the allocation to the military instruction remaining untouched. There was, however, a growing awareness that more time should be given to the practical side of tactical training and a number of outdoor exercises. Again, more time was needed to maintain proper standards in 'the appropriate academic subjects' that were such an important and integral part of the course as a whole.

After much planning and consultation a two-year course was introduced towards the end of 1955. There were now six terms, each of twelve to thirteen weeks, following the pattern of the normal academic year, with a recess at Christmas, Easter, and in the summer. Basic military training occupied the first term, after which the cadet's programme became a

Left *Overseas Training – Exercise Tipperary II, 1958.*

Right *Major General G.C. Gordon Lennox, Commandant RMA Sandhurst 1960–63.*

mixture of military and academic subjects on very much the pre-war pattern that had been adopted in 1947. This two-year course for the Sandhurst entry was endorsed in the findings of a committee presided over by General Sir Lashmir Whistler. The report, dated 1958, at the same time stressed the need for university candidates in the modern Regular Army.

Meanwhile, as regards the Sandhurst course, strong arguments were emerging that better results could be achieved if the instruction in many subjects was more concentrated. These led to further changes in 1961, with the military training largely taking place in the first and last terms, allowing the academic parts of the syllabus to be covered in the intervening terms, but with a third of the time given over to military instruction, including periods in camp or on overseas training. One of the cadets of this period was HRH Prince Michael of Kent, who joined Rhine Company in January 1961, rose to the rank of junior under officer and was commissioned in the 11th Hussars. For all but six months of these two years Rhine was the Sovereign's Company.

The Commandant who implemented these important changes was Major General G.C. Gordon Lennox, CB, CVO, DSO, who as a junior under officer at the RMC had won the King's Medal in 1928. His last appointment before coming to Sandhurst had been GOC 3 Infantry Division. Both his sons had passed through the RMA Sandhurst, being commissioned into the regiment he himself had joined and later commanded, the Grenadier Guards. His eldest son, Bernard, won the Sword of Honour in 1953. With wide experience as a regimental officer and of command, Major General Gordon Lennox was well qualified to set the standards required of an officer cadet, not only on and off the parade ground but also in the classroom, where the new pattern of instruction was to have the greatest effect. By the end of his tour as Commandant the two-year course was well established, and although changes took place under each of his three immediate successors, the basic concept was unaltered.

By 1965 the division of periods had stabilised at 1,403 for the military and 1,076 for the academic parts of the course. Finally, in 1970, a further permutation was introduced. All terms were of fourteen weeks. The military instruction (given 1,755 periods) took place in the first and last two terms, allowing a central 'academic year', in the middle of which one of the two periods of overseas training took place. This academic year was officially described as a foundation year of professionally relevant tertiary education. It had for its basic ingredients, languages, social studies, military technology, mathematics, science, and the modern successor to military history, war studies, the mix being adjusted to meet the requirements of the different Arms of the Service.

A feature of the revised course was the granting of a diploma, based on examination results at the end of the fourth term. On this last point it is

RSM C.H. Phillips with the Old College team in the Pace-Stick Competition (1957). From 1963 to 1970 he held the appointment of Academy Sergeant Major.

significant that in the mid-sixties an independent inquiry into officer education and training in all three Services by Professor Howard and Dr English had recommended, firstly, that cadet training in the cadet colleges should be reduced to a year, and secondly, that after two or three years' service all young officers should attend at least a year's course at a new Joint Services Defence Academy. Their proposal was that this course should count as the first year of any subsequent degree course. When this project was abandoned in 1968, it was hoped, as far as the Army was concerned, that the Sandhurst academic year, carrying the award of a diploma, would serve the same aim. Negotiations with a number of universities, however, failed to get the necessary response, and as we shall see later, a decision had already been taken that was to be a major factor in changing the whole pattern of cadet training at Sandhurst.

From its inception and in the long term the six months' extension of the course to two years could be seen as a necessary insurance for the future. The subsequent alterations in the sequence of the instruction, together with any adjustments to the syllabus, reflected a growing awareness that, under the changing pattern of education in many schools and in the face of the inexorable march of science and technology, educational standards must be kept in balance and broadly based. Again, there were problems that stemmed from the amalgamation and the loss of some of the incentives and competitive rivalry that characterised the smaller, separate, and more closely integrated pre-war cadet establishments. Moreover, for many years the new Academy had been left to make do in overcrowded accommodation and with inadequate facilities, circumstances that, in spite of the acknowledged requirement to cut costs in the long run, had not been envisaged when the decision on amalgamation was taken. Speaking to the first intake in 1947, Major General Matthews had warned the cadets, 'You will not have immediately all the facilities that are planned. To get these takes time, but they are coming on. You will not have the spacious lecture theatres, laboratories, etc., that are planned, and some of your instruction will take place in huts.' For the next fourteen years the science laboratories continued to remain in converted hospital huts, and the building of Victory College and the Churchill Hall was held back for nearly a quarter of a century.

THE 1960s REVIEWED

The inauguration of the Faraday Hall in 1961 was marked by a lecture given by Sir George Thomson, Master of Corpus Christi, Cambridge, a holder of the Faraday Medal of the Institute of Electrical Engineers, in the presence of Lieutenant General Sir Charles Richardson, Director-General of Military Training, and a number of the Arms and Services Directors of the Army Department, together with Dr Davies, the Dean of the Royal Military College of Science, and many others concerned with the project and planning of the building.

A further historic event took place the following year during the Sovereign's Parade in the summer term, to mark the departure of the Academy Sergeant Major from the Sandhurst scene after nearly fifteen years, during which time he had become the senior warrant officer in the Army. John Lord, whose courage, personal example and high standards brought him the respect and admiration of all with whom he came in contact, had been mentor and guide to members of the staff on every level and to the thousands of cadets he had taught. Here, indeed, was a man of truly remarkable qualities whose influence was spread throughout the Service. Her Majesty's representative taking the parade was Admiral of the Fleet Earl Mountbatten of Burma. In his address, having commented on the excellence of the parade, he paid tribute to Mr Lord, 'a great man who retires today after an absolutely outstanding career in the Army'. As the parade drew to its traditional ending, with the Adjutant riding up the steps of the Grand Entrance, the lone figure of the Academy Sergeant Major was seen to move forward to follow across the parade ground and pass through the great doors that would slowly close behind him – an historic and very moving climax.

The Commandant at this time was Major General H.J. Mogg, who had won the Sword of Honour at Sandhurst in 1937. With the number of cadets under instruction showing a gradual rise (to over 1,030 in 1965), and a degree of stability in the pattern and content of the course, there was a growing air of confidence that at last a solution had been found to many earlier problems.

Each term part of the Sovereign's Company Competition was fought out between the twelve companies. The events were: juniors' drill; physical efficiency (swimming, running and PT) in the second term; the assault course in the third term; plus the two company drill competitions and the rifle classification results of the spring and summer terms. Increased emphasis was being given to overseas training and joint exercises with other military academies in NATO, such as Madelon, Blücher and Tipperary. In December 1963, during a winter recess, the Academy ski team won the Inter-Services Cadet Colleges Trophy for the third year running. The event was held at St Moritz, and the trophy was presented by Miss Gina Hawthorn of the British Olympic team. The following year a contingent of cadets again took part in the Edinburgh Tattoo, and throughout the year there was a constant stream of visitors to Sandhurst, Members of

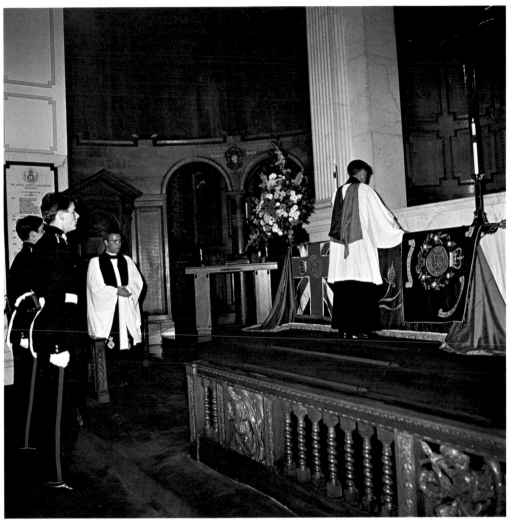

'Colours to Chapel', July 1978. On the last Sunday of term the Colours are placed on the altar at the morning service. From left to right: JUO S.C. Rhodes, JUO E.G. Kelway-Bamber and the Reverend H.L. Jones, Assistant Chaplain. At the altar, the Chaplain, the Reverend C. Rawlinson.

The Sovereign's Parade, April 1979. HRH The Duke of Edinburgh presenting the Sword of Honour to JUO M.R.S. Macrae. On Prince Philip's right is the Commandant, Major General Sir Philip Ward.

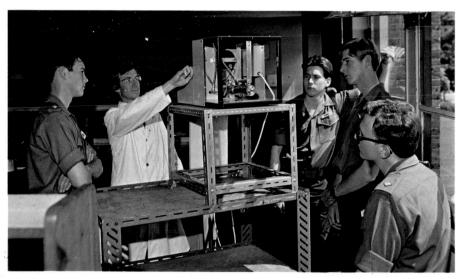

Dr D.L. Jones of the Department of Military Technology demonstrates the rocket motor to student officers attending a laboratory period in the Faraday Hall.

Parliament, representatives of foreign governments, and a spate of senior officers from an increasing number of countries overseas.

Expeditions abroad by organised parties of cadets during the recess were receiving much active support and encouragement. Articles in *The Wish Stream* for 1964 highlighted parties engaged in exploring uncharted areas in south-east Libya, and an overland expedition to an archaeological site near Ankara. Another party, using Klepper double canoes, made the passage over 435 miles of the Danube from Ulm to Vienna, while Captain Blashford-Snell led an expedition to Ethiopia, involving ten cadets and several civilians, to make a collection of wildlife on behalf of the British Museum. During the same summer recess a further fifty cadets were engaged in over a dozen other expeditions – driving from Tangiers to the Aswan Dam and back, or visiting Venezuela and Trinidad, while other parties were travelling to many areas of the Middle East. One party of keen military historians, emulating the 'foot-sloggers' of less sophisticated times, retraced the route followed by Hannibal in crossing the Alps and returned along that taken back from Italy by Napoleon.

For a number of years parachute training during a recess had been a popular activity. The club went by the name of its mascot, Edward Bear, who was an intrepid and regular participant in the jumps. The following account of one of his adventures is related by one of the RAF instructors who knows him well:

In the mid 1960s the OC No. 1 Parachute Training School considered it a sound exercise in Service relationships to run, concurrently, an Edward Bear course and a parachute training course of similar duration for Cranwell cadets. His idea may have been one of co-operation, the cadets, however, decided that it was to be one of intense rivalry. During a well-planned night 'raid' Cranwell cadets stole Edward Bear, returning him to his keeper at breakfast, who had yet to discover his loss. The Sandhurst contingent could not believe that Edward Bear had been returned unharmed – and they were right; under his stitched-down beret was a bare patch bearing a neatly stencilled RAF roundel. The following night two Cranwell cadets 'disappeared'. They reappeared in the middle of crowded Carfax in the centre of Oxford as naked as the day they were born – except for a pair of RMA Sandhurst insignia, neatly stencilled on each 'cheek'.

WAR STUDIES

The study of military history was now under a separate department. Seen as a bridge between the practical and the theoretical elements of the course, the subject was proving increasingly popular with the cadets. The first Reader in Military History, as the head of the department was called, was Professor Boswell, and the syllabus was formulated 'as a study in leader-

*Caving expedition to the French Pyrenees, April 1964. B.S. Gritten, on the left, with
G.N. Heale and E. Smith.*

ship'. When 'Bos' retired in 1959 after thirty-five years at the two
Academies, his successor was Brigadier Peter Young. Here was a man of
many parts, whose exploits as a Commando leader had earned him the
DSO and the MC with two bars, and who was also an historian, an established author and a military commentator of no mean repute. The growing
reputation of the new department attracted a number of young graduates
and several retired regular officers with university qualifications to form a
particularly strong team of lecturers.

Since 1969 this key element in the Sandhurst curriculum has been
under the direction of E.A. Brett-James, who joined the staff in 1961 and is
himself the author of a number of works in the field of military history. He
is now the Head of the Department of War Studies and International
Affairs. The Deputy Head is D.G. Chandler, with J.D.P. Keegan and C.E.
Morris, plus fifteen senior lecturers, covering the respective and closely
linked fields of study. In 1974 a display was mounted in the Library of
published works by members of the staff of the RMA Sandhurst. The
catalogue listed 31 authors and 131 titles. In a foreword John Keegan
wrote:

Sovereign's Parade, July 1967. Field Marshal the Viscount Montgomery and the Commandant, Major General P.M. Hunt, during the inspection.

A great deal of the published work produced at Sandhurst has been military history in the strict sense; but the Military History, together with the Languages and Political and Social Studies Departments, have also made important contributions in the wider field of strategic and associated studies . . . as [has] the Soviet Studies Centre to the study of Communist military affairs.

From serving officers there were works by 'Monkey' Blacker, J.N. Blashford-Snell, Anthony Deane-Drummond, Anthony Farrar-Hockley and W.G.F. Jackson, while ten members of the Military History Department contributed no less than fifty-seven titles.

THE ACADEMY COMES OF AGE

In 1968 the RMA Sandhurst came of age. The Commandant at this date was Major General Hunt, who as General Sir Peter Hunt, GCB, DSO, OBE, was the Chief of the General Staff from 1973 until 1976. He had been commissioned from the RMC in 1935 into the Queen's Own Cameron Highlanders, and his last appointment before returning to Sandhurst as the eighth post-war Commandant was GOC 17 Division and Commander Land Forces Borneo, with added responsibility as Major General Brigade of Gurkhas. He came to Sandhurst at a critical time for the Army as a whole and not least for Sandhurst – we owe him a great debt, for he inspired a sense of stability and high purpose in the face of mounting pressures and an uncertain future.

To glance back to the birth of the RMA Sandhurst, it is appropriate to note that since 1947 over 10,000 British cadets, and 1,100 Commonwealth and foreign cadets from more than 40 different countries, had marched up the steps and through the Grand Entrance of Old College to be commissioned in their respective armies. Of the staff, more than 1,500 officers and instructors had served a tour of duty at the Academy in the twenty-one years of its existence.

In a special number of *The Wish Stream* one contributor, in a passage on 'The Spirit of Sandhurst to Come', felt that 'the new buildings which seem to leap up around us must be the symbol of what is to come. Whatever changes may be ahead, they testify to a continuing activity in Sandhurst to meet new needs.' Another writer recalled that since 1947 six international caps for Rugby had been awarded to ex-cadets (E.M.P. Hardy, D.W. Shuttleworth, J.G. Willcox, C.P. Simpson, G.C. Phipps and J. Mac-Donald) and forty-two caps for Army Rugby. In such terms were the uncertainties of a changing world faced with confidence and pride. The university examination results for the same year showed that twenty-six ex-cadets had been awarded their degrees at eight different universities, while a further forty-five had gained their BSc through the Royal Military College of Science.

At the Sovereign's Parade that summer HRH Princess Alexandra referred to 'the reductions in the size of the Army today [which] mean that three of your famous companies are on parade here for the last time, and although I know that the nine remaining companies will worthily uphold the traditions they have represented, it is sad that the great names of Inkerman, Somme and Normandy must disappear'. On this occasion Senior Under Officer A.G.W. Jackson was presented with both the Sword of Honour and the Gold Medal. For the same cadet to win both awards is exceptional; the only cadets to have gained this distinction since 1947 are:

1948	R.M.H. Vickers	1972	J.C. Brannam
1951	J.F.H. Pease-Watkin	1973	G.F. Lesinski
1956	A.C.D. Lloyd	1973	J.S. Lloyd
1968	A.G.W. Jackson	1976/77	D.B. Simpson*
1969	J.R.M. Hackett	1977/78	P.A. Duncan*
1970	N.C.D. Lithgow		S.M.M. Hughes*

*These awards of the Queen's Medal were for the best student officer on the newly established Regular Career Course.

The RMA Sandhurst contingent parading in the procession at the state funeral of Sir Winston Churchill, 30 January 1965.

Mention should also be made of the exceptional performances of certain Commonwealth cadets: A.L. Crutchley and D.A. Williams, both from Rhodesia, who won the Sword of Honour in 1955 and 1962 respectively, and M.R. Farland from New Zealand, who won the Sword in 1964; also Malik Ghulam Mohd Khan from Pakistan, who won the Queen's Medal in 1960, and G.F. Pearce from New Zealand, who won it in 1968.

The following summer of 1969 HRH The Duke of Edinburgh took the Sovereign's Parade. Here is the central passage of his address:

In times of war and tension people naturally turn their attention to military affairs, but in times of peace and relative security people naturally turn their minds to other matters. Today, universities and business schools are all the rage, yet the Services have had cadet colleges, specialist schools, staff colleges and defence colleges for ages. Today, all great minds are becoming concerned with industrial relations – when the Services learned their lessons generations ago in the much tougher circumstances of war, and they have never ceased to improve their human relations and man-management techniques. Today, there is much discussion about qualifications and career structures, yet the Services have been using comprehensive systems of training, selection and promotion for over fifty years. In fact, the Services are not without experience of mergers and take-overs, and the problems they create.

At this point mention may be made of a recent 'take-over'. For nearly a century, apart from during the Second World War, the Civil Service Commission had conducted the written examination for entry to Woolwich and Sandhurst. This system by which the educational standards on entry had been controlled was now abandoned.

For some years it had been possible for candidates for the RMA Sandhurst to claim exemption from this examination if they possessed five passes in specified subjects in the General Certificate of Education, providing two of these passes were at Advanced Level. In 1964 headmasters were informed that within two years the Commissioners' examination would be discontinued and that the academic standard required for entry to the Academy would be 'GCE passes, or the equivalent, in five approved subjects, which must include English language, mathematics, and either a science or a language other than English. Of these five passes not less than two must normally be at Advanced Level.' The explanation of 'normally' was then given. Candidates offering Ordinary passes in Advanced-Level subjects might be accepted, but the decision would rest with the Sandhurst Entry Board; that is to say 'whether or not [such applicants] are given places will depend on the numbers who are fully qualified and their individual performances at the Regular Commissions Board, at school and in their examinations'.

Any such candidates who failed to obtain a place at Sandhurst might still seek a Short Service Commission, or a Regular sixteen-year Commission, through Mons Officer Cadet School. Furthermore, a candidate who was otherwise recommended as fit for officer training, but 'who appears weak academically', might attend a three-month pre-Sandhurst course at the Army School of Education, Beaconsfield, with a view to being considered either for Sandhurst or for Mons.

Where in this labyrinth was the norm to be found, and how would any scaling-down of educational standards relate to those 'comprehensive systems of training' of which Prince Philip had spoken? Here were problems indeed.

CHAPTER 14

The Challenge Ahead

MOUNTING PRESSURES

In following the progress of Sandhurst and its predecessors over two and a half centuries we have seen many changes. None, not even those of the shortlived 'Sub-Lieutenant Era' in the 1870s, have been so revolutionary as those that have taken place in the last few years. So far we have traced the evolution of the RMA Sandhurst over nearly a quarter of a century, but the hopes and frustrations, progress and setbacks are reflections of a period dominated by a changing international scene, of vacillating policies, of the ending of National Service, of drastic cutbacks in the strength of the Armed Forces and a shrinking economy, in short a slow but inexorable return to the problems long associated with a contracting Service and financial stringency.

There had been a time when the Army itself seemed to be in search of a role; then came the invasion of Czechoslovakia and the civil disturbances in Northern Ireland, so in the early 1970s the further reduction of major Army units was cancelled. But much damage had been done; a number of officers were seeking early retirement and there were fewer candidates for commissions, leaving the Army with an embarrassing shortage of regimental officers. In 1969 the combined output of Sandhurst and Mons was 452, of which the short-service element was 35 per cent; the following year the total was 440, with over 48 per cent having chosen to take the considerably shorter five-month Mons course. Faced with the situation where there were less candidates for entry to the Academy, the Army was relying on a high proportion of short-service officers converting to Regular Commissions and at the same time actively encouraging direct entry from the universities.

Another factor was the question of accommodation for cadet training. Earlier proposals to modernise the Mons Barracks at Aldershot had been turned down on the grounds of cost, and as far back as 1967 the Army Board had decided in principle that the Officer Cadet School should move to Sandhurst. So the idea of 'collocation', as it was termed, was born. But was this solely an economic and administrative expediency, which might

The launching of Wishstream II *in June 1969. In the centre the Commandant, Major General P.T. Tower, watches Mrs Tower launch Sandhurst's new yacht in the traditional manner.*

also save a handful of instructors? Or did it have wider implications, leading to drastic changes in the traditional pattern of cadet training? To locate Mons at Sandhurst, instead of a few miles down the road at Aldershot, could hardly alter the apparent preference of young men for a short course which got them 'on the job' so much more quickly.

POLICIES IN CONFLICT

Early in 1971, with the publication of the Defence Estimates in February, the date of the move of Mons was made public; only one officer-training establishment was now enough for the Army's needs; Mons would move in the autumn of the following year, but would continue to keep its own entity and syllabus. At the same time an announcement came from the Adjutant General that the Director of Military Training had ordered a working party (under Brigadier P.B. Tillard) to review the whole field of officer career training. Having only twelve months earlier launched the refashioned two-year course, the Sandhurst staff were soon to realise that 'collocation' meant not just 'to place together', but also 'to arrange shapes into a pattern', and that there were plans for many shapes and a very different pattern – a pattern indeed that was totally alien to policies advocated by the then Director of Studies, Mr G.S. Sale.

Geoffrey Sale, a distinguished scholar, educationalist and broadcaster, had also represented his county at Rugby and played in the Oxford XV. Joining the staff of Fettes College in Edinburgh in 1931, he remained during the war years to command the OTC and as a housemaster until 1946, when he went to King's School, Bruton, as headmaster. From there he went to take over the headmastership of Rossall School in Lancashire in 1957. Ten years later, on his retirement and in the year that his son passed out from Sandhurst, he was invited to accept the appointment of Director of Studies at the Academy. He had at that time been for eight years a member of the House of Laity in the Church Assembly and on several of its committees, had served on the governing body of two colleges of education and of five schools, including Stonyhurst, and was also a member of the Army Scholarship Boards, RAF Selection Boards and Ordination Selection Boards.

SPORTING SCENE

The Commandant at this unsettling and testing time was Major General P.T. Tower, CB, DSO, MBE, a keen yachtsman and enthusiastic supporter of the many sporting activities that were so much part of the Sandhurst scene. He was the first Commandant of the RMA Sandhurst to have been an instructor at the post-war Academy and the last of the three to have been educated at the Shop. His appointment immediately prior to returning to Sandhurst after an interval of fifteen years was in Aden as the last GOC Middle East Land Forces.

In 1970 the last of the Western European Military Cadets' Athletic Meetings (WEMCAM) was held at Sandhurst. Several records were broken and the Belgians won a fine victory, with the Dutch coming second, a few points ahead of the Academy's team. The Silver Bugle that year was shared between Alastair Riddell, who had broken every Sandhurst record from the 800 metres to the 10 miles and also become the Army and Combined Services Champion at 1,500 metres, and L.K. Sumbeiywo, a brilliant hurdler from Kenya. The following year WEMCAM was replaced by a quite different competition, IMAGE – an Inter-Military Academies Group Exchange. The intense rivalry between the national academies, and presumably a good deal of expense, was avoided by forming small international teams, where each member competed in two events, one athletic, the other either judo, swimming, fencing or pistol. The first of these 'exchange' visits was held in France at the Ecole Polytechnique and proved a highly enjoyable experience for the dozen or so Sandhurst cadets involved.

As far as athletics was concerned, attention now focused on the Triangular Match against Cranwell and Dartmouth, which Sandhurst won by a substantial margin. Ten members of the Academy's team later took part in the Army Individual Championship, gaining no less than seven second or third places, while A.D. Eastgate from Fiji set up a new record in the 100 metres. In the same year M.J. Vacher, riding Paddy, jumped nine consecutive clear rounds at the Royal Tournament to win both the Prince of Wales Cup and the King's Cup, while at Bisley, during the ARA Meeting, J.A.A. Blacker won the Bisley Cup, the NRA Silver Medal, the Archdale Prize and the ARA Silver Spoon.

ALMA MATER

As a result of the review of officer career training, the Army Board announced that everyone commissioned into the Regular Army would in future pass through the RMA Sandhurst. This included any entry from the universities, and as there were also differing types of commissions to be catered for, it was decided that the unifying factor should be a short course modelled on the Mons syllabus. This course in basic military training would lead to an immediate commission, thus enabling young officers to complete their Special to Arm courses and gain experience in the command of soldiers as early as possible.

For the short-service officer there was therefore to be no change in the pattern, but for the former 'Sandhurst' entry seeking a Regular Commission it was decided that some elements of the two-year course should be retained. Having completed the six months' Standard Military Course, these 'student officers' would remain at Sandhurst for a further five months' study on a Regular Career Course. This was to consist of 'Professional Studies', that is war studies and international affairs, military technology, contemporary Britain, and man-management and communication. Thus the former two-year course was compressed into an overall twelve months. But while the new two-tier scheme for cadets seeking a Regular Commission was described as including a 'foundation educational course', there could be no real comparison between the new and the old courses, except in the terminology used. So much had been discarded, including all teaching of languages and mathematics.

Turning to the training of the direct-entry graduates, we find a hybrid potted version of the Military and Professional Studies courses already mentioned. Without going into details of entry through university cadetships and bursaries, which is being increasingly encouraged, it is sufficient to say that all graduate courses at Sandhurst follow this pattern and last about five months.

By the end of 1972 the Academy had been completely reorganised. New

College (initially named Mons College) carried out the basic military training and Old College the professional studies. Of those who passed this Regular Career Course, it was estimated that a third would take an 'in-service' three-year degree course after a spell at regimental duty. Serving officers seeking to convert from a Short Service to a Regular Commission were now required to qualify on this same Regular Career Course. These 'returning officers', many with recent active service experience, form Dettingen Company in Old College. Victory College undertook the courses for graduates, together with the task of preparing a limited number of younger officers of the normal entry who had been selected to go on to take a degree course, but needed some extra qualifications. Victory College was also to run short courses for newly commissioned officers who had been specially recruited, such as chaplains and doctors.

A LIMITED ROLE

Three years previously the Army Board had approved the creation of an Advisory Council, composed of university dons and headmasters from a wide variety of schools and with Professor Michael Howard as chairman,

Filming Young Winston *at Sandhurst in July 1971.*

to advise on the development of the Sandhurst syllabus. The Tillard proposals were in direct conflict with the recommendations of this carefully chosen body of educationalists, not only on the subjects to be taught, the standards to be aimed at, but also on the amount of time that should be devoted to any foundation course. Was the traditional role of Sandhurst as an educational institution for Army officers to be revoked at a stroke? What would now take the place of the lost instruction? Were all long-term plans and projects to be overridden, as in the case of the sudden decision to cancel the rebuilding and enlargement of the Central Library, now holding the most important collection of military works in the United Kingdom outside London and a stock approaching 100,000 volumes? What interpretation should be placed on the Librarian being told by an Establishment Committee that in future there would hardly be any need for a library at all?

Within months of the start of the new courses yet another investigation was announced through a Committee on Army Regular Officer Training, which included as members the Deputy Under-Secretary of State for the Army and the Director of Army Training. Its report was published two and a half years later. Statistics published in the meantime had shown that on average the percentage of commissions gained through the university entry had risen appreciably, and that this trend was particularly noticeable in the case of university cadetships. The number of officers taking degrees after a period of regimental duty had also risen. In endorsing the earlier recommendations of the Tillard Committee it was clear that the Army Board were well satisfied with this situation, for as far as tertiary education for Army officers was concerned, it would be covered in the future by direct recruitment of graduates and through in-service attendance at the Royal Military College of Science and civil universities.

At the same time as this plan was announced the Advisory Council was informed that it would be dissolved. It seems that in the meantime successive Commandants had represented that the tempo of the two main courses, the Standard Military and the Regular Career Course, was too rushed. The latter, for instance, required the whole of the Professional Studies syllabus to be compressed into seventeen and a half weeks without any break and with the student officers working three weekends out of four. The combined twelve months' course for Regular officers was in fact increased to fourteen months early in 1976.

COMPLEXITIES AND PERMUTATIONS

The search for a solution to the problem of officer recruitment in the end produced a system of considerable complexity with a whole host of vari-

202

ables. An official pamphlet, 'Officer Careers in the Army – Methods of Entry', lists no less than nine types of entry, differing educational requirements, ranging from an unspecified qualification through the Army School of Education to a university degree, and at least eight different age brackets for applicants. In the centre of the selection process is the Regular Commissions Board, but on the periphery are ranged other selection boards, such as for university cadetships, and a whole network of regimental interviews, attachments and sponsorships, plus university and school liaison officers, the whole involving many departments in the Ministry of Defence. How different from the pre-war selection process by interview and competitive examination, or the comparable system adopted when the RMA Sandhurst was established, where there was no wide divergence in the ages and educational standards of cadets, and where their relative progress could be assessed through a standard reporting and examination process leading to a final Order of Merit. Have not some of the incentives for study and hard work been removed by the easing of many paths and opening of many doors?

Central to the whole of the training given at Sandhurst is the requirement 'to develop the essential characteristics of leadership and man-management, sense of discipline and sense of duty'. The process is complex and time-consuming and has endless permutations, for as Lord Montgomery pointed out on the subject of leadership training, 'we must analyse the good and bad points in a man's make-up; we must then develop his good points and teach him to keep the bad points in subjection'. Whatever the merits of any particular course or syllabus in other respects, there must be sufficient time for leadership training and the development of those qualities without which the accolade 'Fit to be Commissioned' is meaningless. This training cannot be measured in classroom periods. It involves character-building, a degree of maturity, and the acceptance and practice of responsibility, the opportunity for which is much reduced by the two-tier system and shortness of courses generally.

A MATTER OF STANDARDS

Twenty-five years after the first post-war intake arrived, Major General J.W. Harman, OBE, MC, became the Academy's tenth Commandant. He was no stranger to Sandhurst, having been commissioned from the RMC with the batch that joined in January 1939. His last posting had been as GOC 1st Division, an appointment that his father, the late Lieutenant General Sir Wentworth Harman, had held in the early 1930s. In any process of remoulding, stabilising factors are of great importance. Firm guidance, the lifting of morale, the guarding and forward projection of traditions, these and much else were the daily concern of General 'Jackie', whose quietly confident manner and cheerful friendly presence in class-rooms, and on the training areas and sports fields, brought purpose and direction to the changing scene.

But not all of the Sandhurst scene was changing. Much innate strength remained to support the concept of which Sir John Mogg spoke, when representing Her Majesty at the Sovereign's Parade in December 1972: 'For the first time the Academy will train all our officers to common pro-fessional standards in a bond of unity and friendship which will spread throughout the whole Army, throughout the Commonwealth and our friends from countries overseas.' One might recall that Le Marchant had much the same aim in seeking 'to ground the cadets in science', but by a process where education and training were complementary and proceeded side by side.

At the Sovereign's Parade held in March 1973 there was the unusually large number of 490 cadets passing out, as the last two of the old intakes (51 and 52) and the first of the new Standard Military Courses were all commissioned together. The parade was taken by General Sir Michael Carver, the Chief of the General Staff, who had been commissioned from the RMC in 1935. As he mentioned in his address, he 'had a good deal personally to do with the decision to move Mons, as it was then, here to Sandhurst, and with the subsequent decision to alter the length and conduct of the Regular Commission Course'.

In the same issue of *The Wish Stream* which recorded the full text of this address, the Editor drew attention to the recent noteworthy appointments of two former Commandants and two Assistant Commandants to positions of high responsibility: General Sir John Mogg as Deputy Supreme Allied Commander Europe and General Sir Peter Hunt as the new Chief of the General Staff, while Lieutenant General Sir Cecil Blacker was to take over as Adjutant General and Lieutenant General Sir Harry Tuzo was to be Commander-in-Chief British Army of the Rhine. Of the civilian staff, the retirement was announced of Mr Final, chief cook, after fifty-two years' service, and Mr Goddard, who had for many years been in charge of the Fancy Goods Shop and completed a record fifty-seven years at Sandhurst.

ROYAL RESIDENT

There now seemed to be fewer visitors from overseas, but in June 1973 there was a pleasant 'reunion' when a former member of Normandy Com-pany, General Yakubu Gowan, paid an official visit to make a presentation and set up a fund for 'The Nigeria Prize'. Later in the same month HRH The Princess Anne took the Sovereign's Parade and, though speaking 'as a

The Sovereign's Parade, June 1973. The inspection by HRH
Princess Anne, who is accompanied by the Commandant,
Major General J.W. Harman.

civilian and a female with no claim to being a serving officer', she showed in the most charming manner that she knew a great deal about the Army and what was required of the young men who were about to be commissioned. A few months later everyone at the Academy was delighted and greatly honoured when she and Captain Mark Phillips took up residence in Oak Grove House, on his being posted for a tour of duty as an instructor.

Meanwhile Major General Harman had received a knighthood and been promoted to take command of I Corps in BAOR. His successor as Commandant was Major General R.C. Ford, CB, CBE, who had been commissioned from the RAC OCTU in June 1943 and also been an instructor at the Mons Officer Cadet School, and now returned to Sandhurst after holding the appointment of Commander Land Forces Northern Ireland.

205

It was not long before the Commandant was able to announce that the length of the main courses would be somewhat extended. It had been all too obvious for some time that excessively long terms, overlapping courses and pressures that filled every minute of the day combined to produce an unsatisfactory climate in which to get the best out of students and staff alike, for in this sense 'climate' affects growth as well as the quality of life itself, and temperate conditions are best for both. As the Commandant expressed it, the 'fast concentrated tempo [of the present courses] has proved to be somewhat severe for the more immature candidate and the slower learner, and there has also been too little time to make the best use of the unique facilities which we have at Sandhurst and the special qualities which our high-grade military and academic staff all possess'.

The length of the practical military course became twenty-eight weeks and that of the Professional Studies Course twenty-three weeks, while a week was added to each of the graduate courses. The annual programme was now divided into three terms of fourteen weeks, each ending with a Sovereign's Parade and followed by a proper break. Furthermore, 'in future the aim will be for every cadet and student officer to take a step toward a qualification in one or other of the many adventurous pursuits available during at least one of the breaks which he will have during his time here'. Compared with earlier days, there were still far fewer opportunities for cadets to get away at weekends for such pursuits as climbing, potholing or sailing, but 'adventure training' during any recess now assumed the standing of an officially supported 'growth industry'. For instance, during 1976 a total of 517 cadets and students, plus many of the staff, took part in 26 organised courses, 12 cruises and 9 expeditions in various parts of the United Kingdom and on the Continent. The courses that were held at Joint Service Centres included Unit Expedition Leader, Rock-climbing, Canoeing, Cross-country Skiing, Caving, Subaqua, Off-shore Sailing, Dinghy Sailing and Free-fall Parachuting, a programme which in the following year was considerably extended.

The other change announced by the Commandant concerned the student officers on the Regular Career Course. This was the introduction of the 'Sandhurst Commission', whereby they would still have 'one pip up' (the single star indicating the rank of second lieutenant) but would not be confirmed in a Regular Commission, nor be appointed to a corps or regiment, until the completion of the course. As 'Sandhurst ensigns' they would continue to wear the same badge and order of dress and retain a full identity with the Academy. Gone would be the colourful 'regimentals' which had added a new dimension to Academy parades, to the complete

Major W.H.M. Ross, Scots Guards, Adjutant RMA Sandhurst 1977–79, riding up the steps to the Grand Entrance at the end of the Sovereign's Parade. The custom was originated by Captain F.A.M. Browning, Grenadier Guards, when Adjutant in 1926.

Her Majesty The Queen presenting the Sovereign's Banner to the Royal Military Academy Sandhurst in the forecourt of Buckingham Palace on 27 October 1978.

The Sovereign's Parade, August 1979, at which General Sir Patrick Howard-Dobson, GCB, ADC Gen., represented Her Majesty The Queen. The parade was commanded by Major W.H.M. Ross, Scots Guards.

bewilderment of some onlookers who were already spellbound at the display of mass sword drill.

HER MAJESTY PRESENTS NEW COLOURS

A highlight for all at Sandhurst came in the summer of 1974 when Her Majesty presented new Colours to the Academy. This was the sixth set to be presented since Queen Charlotte's memorable visit some 160 years earlier. Instead of a 'cadet battalion', there were roughly the same number of student officers and officer cadets on parade. In command was the Adjutant, Major J.J.B. Pope, MBE, Coldstream Guards, who had been a cadet on parade when the Queen had presented the old Colours in 1957. In this span of twenty years the Academy had come of age and now faced fresh responsibilities. Here in front of the Old Buildings, for long a symbol of homogeneity and continuity, the time-honoured ceremonial once more was centred on the act of consecration and of personal dedication, as exemplified in the opening words of the Chaplain General, Archdeacon Peter Mallett:

Forasmuch as men in all ages have made for themselves signs and emblems of their allegiance to their rulers, and of their duty to uphold those laws and institutions which God's providence has called them to obey, we, following this ancient and honoured custom, stand before God this day to ask His blessing on these Colours, and to pray that they may be an abiding symbol of our duty towards our sovereign and our country, and a sign of our resolve to guard, preserve and sustain the great traditions of bravery and self-sacrifice of which we are the proud inheritors.

At the conclusion of the service the Queen presented the new Colours, which were received by Second Lieutenant D.N.W. Sewell, Grenadier Guards, and Second Lieutenant D.C. Parkinson, The Parachute Regiment. In her address she spoke of Sandhurst holding a very special place in the history and affections of the British Army, of the importance of strength of character, integrity and moral and physical courage in those who became officers, and Her Majesty concluded with these words:

I am presenting new Colours today as a memorial to the loyal and devoted service of so many of your predecessors, as well as a reminder to you and to those who will follow you that to succeed in the greatest tasks requires the greatest self-sacrifice.

After the final Royal Salute and three cheers for Her Majesty the Colours were marched off. Then came a compliment paid only to the

Sovereign, the march-past of the Sovereign's Platoon with the King George V Banner lowered in salute. Later that afternoon, as the time came for Her Majesty to leave, a huge crowd assembled on the square in front of Old College, generals, ambassadors and senior guests, almost without count, mingling with members of the staff and the parents and friends of the young officers and cadets who were lining the King's Walk, all there to cheer the Queen as she departed. It was a truly memorable occasion and a wonderfully happy day, on which, in the gracious presence of the Queen and the thousands of guests, the best traditions of the Academy had been proudly upheld – an occasion, indeed, which could be said to have demonstrated that 'the whole is greater than the parts'.

In Concert

In the autumn of 1976 Major General Ford was promoted in the appointment of Military Secretary and later received a knighthood in the New Year's Honours. His successor at Sandhurst was Major General Sir Philip Ward, KCVO, CBE, who for the last three years had been GOC London

Jubilee Year Celebrations – Families' Day at Sandhurst, 1 June 1977. The start of the fancy-dress parade.

District and Major General The Household Division. Commissioned into the Welsh Guards in 1943, he had served with the regiment from Normandy until the end of the campaign in North-West Europe. A former Adjutant of the Academy during the years 1960–62, he had earlier held the same appointment at Eaton Hall Cadet School. Other appointments included Brigade Major Household Division, Officer Commanding 1st Battalion Welsh Guards and Commander Land Forces Gulf. Not only did he have personal knowledge of two cadet-training establishments, of many members of the Academy staff and of several generations of cadets, but he had also seen at close quarters and been able to judge the place and value of all that goes to create the Sandhurst ethos. The integration of the staff became a reality and with it a heightened awareness of the standards and objectives demanded by the task in hand.

Early in 1977 a new company was formed. This was Rowallan Company, whose task was to give selected candidates, otherwise acceptable to the Regular Commission Board but as yet too young or rather too immature, a chance of developing their leadership potential. The idea stemmed from the Highland Fieldcraft Training Centre run during the Second World War by Lord Rowallan, and the ten-week course makes use of various forms of adventure training, similarly designed to inculcate mental tough-ness and physical self-reliance. This scheme has undoubtedly proved of value under the present organisation and with courses of the present length, yet it adds a further dimension to an already complex, piecemeal and polarised process, the growth of which, it could be said, might be better regulated in the long term by a balanced diet, rather than by a series of injections.

As regards the Regular Career Course, there has been a small but impor-tant adjustment. After a complete abandonment of all languages instruc-tion for five years, a slot in the syllabus has been made so that French, German or Russian may be taken as a voluntary option by a limited number of students who have already obtained the appropriate 'O'-Level qualifica-tion. Owing to the dismemberment of the Language Department, however, there are at present few qualified lecturers, and in the short time available the teaching can only aim at a small number of officers reaching a colloquial standard.

MEDALS AND OTHER AWARDS

When the two-year course ended and Sandhurst was faced with conducting a number of short courses at differing levels many of the awards and prizes, especially those that had been given for academic subjects, were no longer appropriate. Some were reallocated, some simply disappeared, and in certain cases new awards had to be initiated. An example of the latter was the Commandant's Medal, which was introduced in 1973 at the suggestion of Colonel Nigel Frend who commanded Victory College. The proposal was that a medal should be awarded to the student officer on each Post University Cadetship Course and each Direct Entry Graduate Course who was considered by the Commandant to be the best of his course. The medal is of silver with the Sandhurst badge in the centre surrounded by the inscription 'Awarded by the Commandant'. The first student officer to receive the medal was a former university cadet, Second Lieutenant A.J.M. Durcan Gordons, while the first award for a Direct Entry Course student went to Second Lieutenant J. Orme, RTR, in the following year.

In May 1977 the Commandant directed that the award of the Sword of Honour should be reserved for the best Regular or Special Regular Commission candidate on the Standard Military Course and that the best Short Service Commission candidate should be awarded a Commandant's Medal. The first to receive the medal under these conditions was Junior Under Officer A.D.R. Windham on Course 14, and the medal was presented by HRH The Duke of Kent at the Sovereign's Parade in August. The Sword of Honour on this occasion went to Junior Under Officer P.A. Duncan, and the Overseas Award for the best overseas cadet on the course was won by Cadet Corporal G.H. Noori from Iraq. In the following year, however, it was decided that the Sword of Honour would again be awarded to the best officer cadet on each Standard Military Course, regardless of his type of commission. So, apart from A.D.R. Windham, only three other officer cadets have won the Commandant's Medal: J.P. Winser, J.J.C. Bucknall and E.G. Kelway-Bamber.

Prizes for academic work and for the top students qualifying for certain of the Arms are now awarded only for the Regular Career Courses. Compared with earlier times there are far fewer subjects involved in the strictly limited Professional Studies Courses, and it is sad to note that many of the traditional awards are no longer applicable and the achievements of several distinguished former cadets no longer commemorated through awards bearing their names.

While some old links have gone, new ones have taken their place. Notably there are three special prizes for overseas student officers on each Regular Career Course. These are the Nigeria Prize, for the best officer, the HRH Prince Saud Abdul Abdullah Faisal Prize for War Studies and International Affairs, and the Brunei Award for the best contribution to extra-mural activities. Of the overseas student officers on Regular Career Course No. 12 who completed their professional studies in the summer of 1977, Second Lieutenant W.A. Sutherland from Jamaica received both the

The Oman Hall, the recently built indoor sports centre for Sandhurst, showing men of the Demonstration Company from the 1st Battalion 2nd KEO Goorkha Rifles using the excellent facilities.

Nigeria Prize and the Brunei Award, while the Prince Faisal Prize was won by Second Lieutenant C.P. Chew from Singapore. It is of interest that on the next three courses the Nigeria and the Prince Faisal Prizes were both won by the same overseas officers, Second Lieutenant C.S. Seath from Singapore, Second Lieutenant F.N. Osokogu from Nigeria and Second Lieutenant W.W. Siak from Singapore. Siak had the distinction of being the first overseas officer on any Regular Career Course to be placed first in academic studies, being awarded the Narrien Cup and the Director of Studies First Prize for 'meritorious performance in academic professional studies as a whole'.

A Broader View

The Chief of the General Staff in 1977 was General Sir Roland Gibbs, GCB, CBE, DSO, MC, who had been an instructor at Sandhurst in 1949 and 1950. Addressing the Academy on a Sovereign's Parade, he concluded with the following words:

Britain's future, and in consequence her major military commitment, lies in Europe and the NATO Alliance. The rapid and continuing expansion of Soviet

213

military capabilities makes the success of this alliance synonymous with the survival of Western European democracy. To some extent this means that national pride must be subordinated to European cohesion and you will be required to become something much closer to European citizens than any of your predecessors and to co-operate in much fuller measure with other nations of the Alliance. You will have to cast off traditional British insularity and reticence to make an impact upon a worthwhile contribution to the collective security of Western Europe.

From all I have said, you will realise that the attainment of your commissions is but the first hurdle of a series. You have already achieved a great deal, but much will be expected of you yet. The challenge awaits you and, formidable though it may seem, you would not be standing here today were the Army not confident of your ability to meet it. Good luck to you all and God speed.

But what of this 'first hurdle' and the challenge it poses for Sandhurst itself? Certainly it should not be seen in isolation, and in a changing world it is the long-term view that is important. Speaking nearly thirty years ago, Field Marshal Montgomery, the then Chief of the Imperial General Staff, defined the task of the RMA Sandhurst as being 'to produce an officer who will be fit morally, mentally and physically to lead the British soldier'. Where standards are involved, there can be no equivocation and time must be allowed for their full achievement in every particular. Just as the height of the 'first hurdle' should be related to others that will follow, so should the standards for entry to Sandhurst measure the ground that must already have been covered, as it is the gaps between these two points and sets of standards that will have to be filled. This is the equation that has to be resolved before the content and length of any Sandhurst course can be determined.

This short history of the RMA Sandhurst and its predecessors has attempted to trace an evolutionary process that has extended over many years, to show the pattern of change, the emergence of traditions and something of the making of policies and the facing of many problems. In passing it may also have pointed to some lessons learned in the past that have significance in our own times.

Epilogue

On 27 October 1978 the King George V Banner was lowered in salute to the Sovereign for the last time. A few moments later Her Majesty Queen Elizabeth presented a new Banner in its place, which is to be known as the Sovereign's Banner. The guard of honour which was mounted for this historic occasion was found as follows: Commanding the Guard, Sandhurst Ensign B.L. Eckett; Lieutenant, Sandhurst Ensign C.R. Prince; Ensign for the King George V Banner, Cadet Corporal M.G.R. May; Ensign to receive the Sovereign's Banner, Cadet Corporal T. Breitmeyer; and one hundred officer cadets; and the following warrant officers: Academy Sergeant Major R.P. Huggins, MBE, Grenadier Guards, and Regimental Sergeant Major R.O. Barnes, Grenadier Guards.

The ceremony took place in the forecourt of Buckingham Palace in the presence of TRH The Prince and Princess Michael of Kent, the Chief of the General Staff General Sir Roland Gibbs, together with members of the Army Board, former commandants and a representative gathering of past and present members of the staff of the RMA Sandhurst and their wives. A special guest was the Marquess Camden who, as Under Officer the Earl of Brecknock, had received the George V Banner from His Majesty on the same spot sixty years previously. In the Mall, beyond the Palace railings, a large crowd pressed in on all three sides to watch the ceremony and listen to Her Majesty's speech and the reply made on behalf of the Academy by Cadet Corporal Breitmeyer. The Queen spoke as follows:

In 1918 my grandfather King George V presented to Sandhurst a Banner which was always to be carried by the Champion Company on parade.

I have seen the painting of that scene and it must have been a memorable occasion. Only four days before the declaration of the Armistice the King was paying a remarkable compliment to the Royal Military College by giving them a personal Banner, and by performing the ceremony in front of his home in the heart of London. The nation owed a great debt to the College and this was being acknowledged by the King on behalf of everyone.

Sandhurst had made an outstanding contribution to our country by training so many of the officers for the First World War. This tradition has been carried on ever since, and the Royal Military Academy continues today to provide the officers for the finest professional army in the world.

Times have changed and Sandhurst has undergone many reorganisations; but my grandfather's Banner has been carried on every major parade since it was presented. More recently it has been the privilege of the Champion Platoon to carry the Banner. From today I would like this Platoon to be known as the Sovereign's Platoon, in keeping with the custom started by my father in 1948.

My grandfather's hope was that his Banner should be looked upon as an emblem of honour. We have only to look at the record of service of the officers who have come from Sandhurst in the last sixty years to realise that the hope he expressed on that day in 1918 has been more than fulfilled.

I now entrust this Sovereign's Banner to the Sovereign's Platoon, being confident that they and their successors will always carry it in the sure knowledge that they are the best from this splendid Military Academy.

Here indeed was history in the making – a royal occasion to be long remembered. We have also looked back to an earlier age when the Royal Military Academy was established by King George II 'to form good officers of Artillery and perfect Engineers', as well as to Sandhurst's formative years under Le Marchant, when King George III spoke of the Royal Military College as 'an object of the deepest national importance'. The Royal Military Academy Sandhurst is not only the inheritor of this trust, it has the added responsibility of being our only academy for officers of the Army; as such, its continued growth and development in our own times require to be doubly ensured.

Appendix

Succession of Commandants, Assistant Commandants, Directors of Studies, Adjutants, and Regimental and Academy Sergeant Majors of the Royal Military Academy Sandhurst, 1946–1979, with dates of appointment.

COMMANDANTS

Maj. Gen. F.R.G. Matthews, DSO	June 1946
Maj. Gen. H.C. Stockwell, CB, CBE, DSO	June 1948
Maj. Gen. D. Dawnay, DSO	January 1951
Maj. Gen. R.G.S. Hobbs, DSO, OBE	February 1954
Maj. Gen. R.W. Urquhart, DSO	November 1956
Maj. Gen. G.C. Gordon Lennox, CB, CVO, DSO	January 1960
Maj. Gen. H.J. Mogg, CBE, DSO	April 1963
Maj. Gen. P.M. Hunt, DSO, OBE	January 1966
Maj. Gen. P.T. Tower, CB, DSO, MBE	August 1968
Maj. Gen. J.W. Harman, OBE, MC	February 1972
Maj. Gen. R.C. Ford, CB, CBE	November 1973
Maj. Gen. Sir Philip J.N. Ward, KCVO, CBE	October 1976
Maj. Gen. R.M.H. Vickers, MVO, OBE	September 1979

ASSISTANT COMMANDANTS

Designated Chief Instructor:

Col. (later Brig.) M.S.K. Maunsell, DSO, OBE	July 1946
Brig. J.C. Walkey, CBE	July 1949
Brig. G.B. Bell, CBE	June 1951

Designated Assistant Commandant (from 1952):

Brig. F.C.C. Graham, DSO	August 1953
Brig. D.S. Gordon, CBE, DSO	January 1956
Brig. G.L.W. Andrews, DSO	November 1957
Brig. C.H. Blacker, OBE, MC	April 1960
Brig. H.C. Tuzo, OBE, MC, BA	June 1962
Brig. A.J. Deane-Drummond, DSO, MC	October 1963
Brig. J.H.S. Read, OBE, MA	May 1966
Brig. G.R. Flood, MC	August 1968

Brig. J.H. Page, OBE, MC   February 1971
Brig. P.J. Bush, OBE   February 1974
Brig. J. Whitehead, MBE   August 1976
Brig. W.H. Allen   March 1979

DIRECTORS OF STUDIES
H.H. Hardy, CBE, MBE, MA   August 1946
T.S.J. Anderson, CBE, TD, MA   September 1948
J.W. Taylor, OBE, TD, MA (Acting)   January 1962
K. Ingham, OBE, MC, MA, D.PHIL, FIAL   May 1962
T.N. Allen, MC, TD, MA (Acting)   May 1967
G.S. Sale, MA, FRSA   September 1967
T.N. Allen, MC, TD, MA (Acting)   September 1971
B.J. Moody, MA, FRIC   January 1972
D. Moss, MA   September 1973

ADJUTANTS
Capt. (later Maj.) The Earl Cathcart, DSO, MC, SG   August 1946
Maj. C. Earle, DSO, OBE, Gren Gds   December 1947
Maj. V. F. Erskine Crum, CIE, MC, SG   January 1951
Maj. A.B. Mainwaring-Burton, IG   February 1954
Maj. J.W. Scott, Gren Gds   December 1955
Maj. D.A.H. Toler, MC, Coldm Gds   August 1958
Maj. P.J.N. Ward, WG   July 1960
Maj. J. Swinton, SG   August 1962
Maj. M.A.P. Mitchell, Coldm Gds   September 1964
Maj. G.A. Allan, IG   September 1966
Maj. M.W.F. Maxse, Coldm Gds   December 1968
Maj. D.V. Fanshawe, Gren Gds   September 1970
Maj. J.J.B. Pope, MBE, Coldm Gds   November 1973
Maj. R.J.S. Corbett, IG   November 1975
Maj. W.H.M. Ross, SG   December 1977

REGIMENTAL SERGEANT MAJORS
RSM A.J. Brand, MVO, MBE   October 1946
RSM J.C. Lord, MBE   July 1948
RSM W.L.A. Nash   May 1955
RSM J.C. Lord, MBE   March 1956

Appointment redesignated:
ACADEMY SERGEANT MAJORS
AcSM J.C. Lord, MVO, MBE   December 1960
AcSM C.H. Phillips, MBE   August 1963
AcSM R.P. Huggins, MBE   December 1970

Selected Bibliography

UNPUBLISHED MATERIAL

Military papers and correspondence of General Le Marchant; letter-books and documents held in the Central Library archives and the Sandhurst Collection of the RMA Sandhurst.

PUBLISHED MATERIAL

Books

Bond, Brian, *The Victorian Army and the Staff College, 1854–1914* (Eyre Methuen, London, 1972). Opening chapters.

Buchanan-Dunlop, Lieutenant Colonel H.D., *Records of the Royal Military Academy, 1741–1892*, second edition (Royal Artillery Institution, Woolwich, 1893).

Experienced Officer, An, *Complete Guide to the Junior and Senior Departments of the Royal Military College* (London, 1849).

Godwin-Austen, Major A.R., *The Staff and the Staff College* (Constable, London, 1927). Opening chapters.

Guggisberg, Captain F.G., '*The Shop': The Story of the Royal Military Academy* (Cassell, London, 1900).

Harries-Jenkins, Gwyn, *The Army in Victorian Society* (Routledge and Kegan Paul, London, 1977).

Hogg, Brigadier O.F.G., *The Royal Arsenal: Its Background, Origins and Subsequent History*, Volume I (Oxford University Press, London, 1963).

Hogg, Brigadier O.F.G., *The Royal Military Academy in the 18th Century* (Society of Antiquaries, London, 1953).

Le Marchant, Denis, *Memoirs of the Late Major General Le Marchant* (London, 1841).

Maurice-Jones, Colonel K.W., *The Shop Story, 1900–1939* (Royal Artillery Institution, Woolwich, 1955).

Mockler-Ferryman, Lieutenant Colonel A.F., *Annals of Sandhurst: A Chronicle of the Royal Military College from its Foundation to the Present Day, with a Sketch of the History of the Staff College* (Heinemann, London, 1900).

Smyth, Brigadier Sir John, *Sandhurst: The History of the Royal Military Academy, Woolwich, the Royal Military College, Sandhurst, and the Royal Military Academy Sandhurst, 1741–1961* (Weidenfeld and Nicolson, London, 1961).

Thomas, Hugh, *The Story of Sandhurst* (Hutchinson, London, 1961).

Thoumine, R.H., *Scientific Soldier: A Life of General Le Marchant, 1766–1812* (Oxford University Press, London, 1968).

Royal Commissions and Parliamentary Inquiries concerning Officer Education and the Cadet Colleges

Select Committee on the Royal Military College, Sandhurst, Parliamentary Paper 317 (1855).

Report on the Training of Officers for the Scientific Corps, together with an Account of Foreign and Other Military Education (HMSO, 1857).

Report of the Royal Commission on the Present State of Military Education and the Training of Candidates for Commissions in the Army (HMSO, 1868–70).

Report of the Committee Appointed to Enquire into the Entrance Examinations (in Non-Military Subjects) of Candidates for Commissions in the Army (HMSO, 1894).

Report of the Committee Appointed to Consider the Education and Training of Officers of the Army (HMSO, 1902) – The Akers-Douglas Committee.

Report of the Committee on the Education and Training of Officers (Cmd 2031, 1924) – The Haldane Committee.

Journals

RMA Magazine (1900–39).

RMC Record (1912–39).

The Wish Stream: Journal of the Royal Military Academy Sandhurst (1947–).

Index

ILLUSTRATION ACKNOWLEDGEMENTS

The drawing on page 13 is reproduced by gracious permission of Her Majesty the Queen.

SOURCES OF ILLUSTRATIONS

Barratts Photo Press, London 193; Chris Bonington 179; Colonel H.N. Clowes 148, 150; Crookshank Collection, RMA Sandhurst 40; Ron Francis, Camberley 135, 136 top, 136 bottom, 153 top, 153 bottom, 169, 177, 178, 190 bottom, 213; R. Goodall 171 top, 172, 189; Keith Hamshere 201; Wing Commander J.H. Hoskins 138; Imperial War Museum, London 125, 151, 156, 157; D.L. Lloydlangston 192; Marshall's, Camberley 190 top, 207 top, 208; National Army Museum, London 28, 198; Public Relations HQ United Kingdom Land Forces 205; Public Relations HQ London District 207 bottom; RMA Sandhurst Collection 31, 34–5, 42, 44, 49 top, 49 bottom, 50 top, 50 bottom, 53, 55, 67 top, 67 bottom, 68 top, 68 bottom, 71, 73, 75, 79, 93, 97, 108–9, 110, 118, 120, 142, 154 top, 154 bottom, 159, 161, 165, 166, 174, 180, 182, 183, 184, 186, 195; *RMC Record* 57, 145; *Records of the RMA* 16, 19, 36, 52; Major E.J.R. Rose 210; Royal Artillery Institution 62, 85, 88, 90, 103, 114, 117, 132; R. Snailham 171 bottom; Hay Wrightson 185.

Items from the Royal Artillery Institution, the RMA Sandhurst Collection, the Crookshank Collection RMA Sandhurst, *Records of the RMA* and the *RMC Record* and those reproduced on pages 23 and 25 were photographed by Ron Francis, R. Goodall, Marshall's and Pace.